The Engaged Parish:

A Practical Guide to Creating a Community of

Spiritual Discernment

By Robert Choiniere, D.Min.

To all the giants

on whose shoulders I stand

Table of Contents

Introduction – Why I write

When I was growing up, our family moved several times. After unloading the truck and unpacking the boxes, the priority was to seek out the local parish. My brother and I would present our credentials as qualified altar boys, and my mother would enroll us in CCD. As a result of these moves, I received my sacraments in different parishes. I was baptized in Vermont but received my First Communion in Florida. We moved to northern Pennsylvania where children were confirmed in 3rd grade, but I was already in 6th grade. Finally, when I was a teenager, we moved one last time. Upon registering at the parish, my brother immediately entered confirmation class with the other 8th graders, but at 16, there was no place for me. I had missed the confirmation window. The pastor then recommended that I join the class of adults joining the church.

My mother would bring me to the evening class each week, where I joined a group of adults discussing their budding faith. They learned about the church, not through workbooks or school-like lessons but through conversation and questions. There were sometimes disagreements and confusion, but just as often, there were realizations and connections. People spoke earnestly and with importance about their lives and what this faith meant to them. I was invited to tell my story. I articulated for the first time why I wanted to be Catholic.

These adults, who started as strangers, quickly became friends. They were interested in me. They listened intently to my thoughts about the church and my experiences. My one singular view of the Catholic faith expanded as I listened to the stories of people discerning a deliberate choice to join the church after sensing a call, each in a unique way.

After our formation, we gathered to hold what our teacher, the deacon, called an Agape Meal. He brought a round loaf of fresh bread, which I imagined Jesus used. He poured wine into cups that we formed into the shape of a fish on the table. He blessed the bread and passed it around as we each tore a piece, held it, and looked at each other, each of these friends who had been strangers just six months earlier. After reading scripture and reflecting on our time together with laughter and tears, we ate the bread and shared a full potluck meal. This group of people felt more like family. We had come to know each other profoundly as we learned about the God who had been calling each of us our entire lives. This family of faith also helped me find conviction in my beliefs as I said out loud what mattered to me and how I wanted to serve the mission of Jesus in tangible, concrete ways. The commitments I said out loud that evening have remained with me my entire life. That experience of a learning community of faith, engagement, belonging, commissioning, and support launched me on a path toward professional lay ministry in the Church.

I have spent the past 25 years supporting and encouraging Catholic parishes to become more grounded in similar experiences of engagement and transformation. An Engaged Parish is a community that learns together how the Spirit of the living Christ is alive in their midst and hearts and how to follow and trust in it. They do this by becoming more deeply grounded in their faith, more connected to one another, and aware and responsive to the world's needs.

This book is meant as a conversation starter to assist pastors, deacons, parish ministers, religious educators, and Catholic leaders consider some marks and practices of an engaged community that trusts in the Spirit to direct their decisions and actions and what it would mean to follow this way.

Chapter One

Does the Church change?

As a young diocesan minister in Brooklyn, New York, I was charged with introducing strategic planning in every parish in the diocese. Many pastors were suspicious of this new initiative. Some were openly hostile. I visited a long-tenured pastor at his rectory to understand this perspective.

I lamented, "Father, I do not understand why more pastors are not embracing change as their parishes are declining rapidly, and planning together could be helpful."

He looked at me amusingly, breathed a long, dramatic sigh, and answered, "Robert, how long have you been here and still have not figured it out?"

Sensing I was about to learn a closely guarded secret of the resistance, I leaned in, waiting for the answer to his own question.

"A Brooklyn pastor wakes up in the morning to make sure things don't change."

Many Catholics and non-Catholics regard the church as unchanging, a solid, immutable foundation in a rapidly shifting world. A static stance provides security, surety, and grounding in an otherwise liquid society seemingly addicted to novelty and change for change's sake. Church leaders act as repositories of the one singular and always constant answer. From this firmly rooted foundation, they offer a single and correct perspective. Seminary formation equips clergy with the only correct Catholic interpretation and understanding of scripture, tradition, human experience, and world affairs.

Members of the church find consistency is the bedrock of faith and assurance that this perspective will never change. Conclusions about every facet of human nature had been reached centuries ago. The questions no longer require litigation or support from existential evidence. On the contrary, all experience is interpreted through fixed lenses. God revealing something new through experience is foreign and a threat to the credibility of sure faith. There is no process for testing anything new. God doing new things is contrary to the very definition of God. God is the unmoved and decoded point of stability and firmness. Leadership requires only reiteration.

Is it possible or credible for the universal Church, local communities, or individual disciples to learn new things from God? Could our understanding of God's desire grow? Can God do something new?

Before ascending to the Father, Jesus says, "I am with you always, until the end of the age."[1] This is a source of great comfort and encouragement, recognizing that Christ is still present and living within the community of faith. But how does this happen? Did Jesus mean that his words are with us in the Gospel, and we can refer back to them? No, Catholic theologians and mystics have been clear throughout the tradition that Jesus Christ is a living presence in the hearts of believers and the community. Christ alive is literal, not in just a figurative or literary sense. If true, how is Christ communicating to the Church now? How do Catholic communities and disciples engage the living Christ? What new understandings might be revealed if we do?

Dei Verbum, the Dogmatic Constitution on Divine Revelation from the Second Vatican Council, offers some insight on this point:

---

[1] Mt. 28:20

"The Tradition that comes from the Apostles **makes progress** in the Church with the help of the Holy Spirit. There is a **growth in insight** into the realities and words that are being passed. This comes about through the contemplation and study of believers who ponder these things in their hearts. It comes from the intimate sense of spiritual realities which they **experience**. Thus, as the centuries go by, **the Church is always advancing** toward the plentitude of divine truth until eventually, the words of God are fulfilled in it.[2]

Dei Verbum speaks eloquently of development, advancement, and progress as essential to the Church's nature. Growth and newness denote the Christian life. The document assures us that there are new things to be learned. This growth comes from believers who "ponder these things in their hearts" and reflect on their experience. Only in this way do we advance and move towards truth. Dei Verbum lays the task in our hands. It

---

[2] Dei Verbum, 8.

does not give us a complete handbook but a directive to reflect, study, and contemplate together. The challenge is learning to do this faithfully, honestly, and with courage. As people on the way, our actions are rooted in complete trust in the Spirit. Moving from a static to a progressive reality means relying on different indicators to measure fidelity. In addition, new practices are needed to mine the open field of experience for the buried treasure of divine inspiration just waiting to be revealed.

At the same time, Dei Verbum clearly states that Scripture and Tradition are foundational to understanding God's revelation. The advancement and progress of the Church is found in adherence to the prophets and the Gospel. The question is not a polarity between unmoored progress and unchanging stability. Instead, the Christian faith is always tethered to tradition while growing and developing without becoming stuck in any historical epoch. This is not change for change's sake but a progression toward the Reign of God, whose goals will always be justice, peace, and salvation. Yet, there will always be more to understand. There are always new ways emerging. The method of perceiving these new ways begins with listening for the revelation of God in scripture and experience.

The role of a leader in a community of growth differs from one rooted in static surety. The pastor's mission is not "to make sure things don't change" but to facilitate the authentic discernment of the Holy Spirit, encourage deep listening to scripture and their experience, push towards the margins, seek consensus, and support discerned action. In this leadership model, pastors and parish leaders can say, "My job is to make sure that things keep changing here." The Spirit always presses forward, calling the body of Christ to follow with trust and faith in this call. How can this be done authentically? What are the risks of following this call? What are the risks of standing still?

Chapter Two

Engaging the Vertical and Horizontal

'You shall love the LORD your God with all your heart, and with all your soul, and with all your mind.' This is the great and foremost commandment. The second is like it, 'You shall love your neighbor as yourself.' (Matt 22:36-39)

An engaged parish finds its root and creative tension at the vertical and horizontal intersections of the church's mission and self-understanding. A helpful physical expression is an outline of a Gothic cathedral. From the foundations to the vaulted ceilings, the altar to the stained glass, gothic cathedrals are embodied symbols intended to convey a deeper theological understanding of Christian beliefs. The very outline is a cross, the central symbol of Christianity formed by the intersection of a vertical and horizontal field. The space itself invites reflection on the meaning of the cross for the community that gathers within it. While always representing the central theological mystery of Christ's suffering and death, a cross reveals a primary dimension of the church's self-understanding.

The Christian community facilitates a vertical relationship between God and God's people and invites and deepens a horizontal relationship among community members. The heart of the Church's mission is attending to both dimensions and drawing them together at an intersection. This intersection was galvanized by Jesus when he equated the two greatest commandments – love of God and love of others. The Church must do both simultaneously. The goal of an Engaged Parish is to deepen the vertical relationship with God and the horizontal relationships with others.

Each Christian community exists to connect people to God through sacraments and scripture. The parish is where the love relationship between God and God's people can be lived and deepened. Parish leaders mediate this relationship by teaching people how to love and know God more deeply. They communicate and demonstrate God's love in both words and actions. Listening to the word of God in the Scriptures is central to nurturing this relationship with what St. Benedict called the "ear of our heart" and responding.

This deep engagement requires practice, attention, and a firm commitment to being open to what God is saying. As the relationship develops, a disciple might be able to say with complete openness, like King David, "Speak, Lord, for your servant is listening"[3] ready for whatever might come. This trustful engagement is transformative as disciples are attuned to this voice and courageously follow it. This level of engagement requires patience, trust, and surrender.

The parish is a training ground where each disciple and the entire community learn how to listen and respond to God, forever speaking to the ear of their hearts.

However, this vertical dimension of the church can become distorted when cut off from others. Jesus is quick to point out in Matthew's gospel that loving our neighbor as ourselves "is like" (some translations even say "is the same") as the first commandment to love God. Again and again, Jesus points out negative examples of people who seemingly love God but do not seem interested in loving their neighbor or anyone else, from the priest and Levite in the Parable of Good Samaritan (Lk. 10:25-37) to the

---

[3] I Samuel 3:9

Pharisee and tax collector (Luke 18:9-14) or the story of the one who stores up grain (Luke 12:16-21) to the rich man and Lazarus (Luke 16:19-31). There are so many references to the folly of not connecting the horizontal to the vertical that it is impossible to conceive of being a disciple of Jesus without caring for others.

Therefore, the horizontal nature of the church is as essential as the vertical. Relationships with other disciples in the community are a hallmark of Christianity, central to its very nature, as critical as the vertical relationship with God. We learn something about God by loving others. Within the Christian community, listening is a central way to engage and deepen the horizontal experience of the Church.

Listening to others, especially in our faith community, is an opportunity to learn what God is doing. This first requires an open space of receptivity to take in the sacred story of another person without prejudice or preconceived ideas. Deep listening and open sharing require patient practice. The parish community is a training ground where people can learn to tell their sacred stories and listen to others. Listening for the presence of Christ alive in another person's experience develops the ability to discern God's voice in one's own life. We help each other become more attuned to God's presence in our experience and the world.

But the Church can never be flattened only to a horizontal plane. If it does, the Church is reduced to a social club connecting members. Eliminating the vertical dimension of the church's mission may seem ridiculous. How could that ever happen? Yet, when the church fails to act prophetically, when the call to transformation through service is brushed aside, or when members doubt or deny their connection with the animating Spirit, then the vertical relationship of the Church suffers. There may be the appearance of a vertical engagement, but its character becomes dull and rigid. When authentic open listening stops, a community can go through the motions of a vertical relationship but be unmoved by the words they proclaim or transformed by the sacraments they celebrate. Such a community becomes a place where members gather to reinforce their connections, but even these lose their depth as surface decoration or simple social cohesion becomes central.

An engaged parish is a place of encounter with God transmitted through sacrament, scripture, and community.

God's words and presence in the community and our lives can have no effect without listening. Listening is critical to cultivating intimacy with God. God is always speaking using any means possible. This divine communication is all around us. Each Christian community is a reservoir of divine experience waiting and wanting to be tapped. Learning how to listen to one another with the ear of our heart, reflecting on Scripture and the signs of the times, and discerning a response enables the intersection of the horizontal and vertical intersection to be a place of deep and lasting conversion and transformation from brokenness to new life.

Against the Flat and Self-Referential

Many people lack depth in their lives. They do not acknowledge a transcendent reality broader than their empirical senses or more profound than their immediate sensations. There is a flatness to contemporary experience. An understanding that this is all there is. What you can see and feel is the only reality that exists. There is nothing more significant or profound to which we are connected. Any vertical relationship is an illusion.

The opposite of the horizontal extension is a self-referential life. People are good in as much as they contribute to my wants and desires. Every person is measured according to self-interest. People are irrelevant or burdensome if they interfere with my interests and desirable and valuable if they can satisfy me. My life is simply about me. The measure of everyone and everything else in the created order is judged according to its help or hindrance to my life.

The cruciform life is in stark contrast to a flat and self-referential existence. It stretches up and down and out and wide to see the universe, ourselves, and every created thing as charged with a divine, engaged, and loving presence.

This practical, empirical mindset can also infiltrate parishes and faith communities. The result is disengagement from one another and God. When parishes focus only on the external forms without inviting disciples to the inner realities, the richness and depth of the Christian faith can become flat. A parish can have beautiful structures, perfectly organized committees, precise schedules, and all signs of a healthy organization. Still, parish life can become sterile and soulless without an

engagement with the living God. An engaged parish is not defined necessarily by an abundance of activity or a higher percentage of participation. Engagement means that community members actively pursue their spiritual growth and development; they are stretched vertically and given the tools and support to journey to their core. An engaged parish is filled with mentors and models ready to guide disciples into the depth of their interiority and offer authentic encounters of shared humanity where their gifts and presence can be transformed and transformative.

There is a hunger in the human spirit for God, but this God is not a product packaged by the Church. An external commodity does not fill spiritual hunger. The hunger is for spiritual depth. The sacraments, traditions, and scriptures are meant to nurture the connection and foster the relationship between each disciple and the God that resides at their very core. When this connection is made, the result always pushes the individual beyond themselves in service and generosity towards greater empathy, compassion, and love since this is the nature of God.

Seen this way, the parish is a gathering of disciples who support one another on a spiritual journey of depth and breadth. How can parishes support the journey and remain grounded in the living God that animates all and each?

When the parish priority is the spiritual journey of all and each, a new lens is formed, and new questions emerge. How do we engage each parishioner in their spiritual journey? How do we encourage people to explore their spiritual depths and relationship with the living God? How are we providing opportunities for people to accompany one another on this journey? How do we provide opportunities for people to offer their gifts and exercise their discipleship in meaningful ways? How do we determine how God is calling us as a community to be the presence of Christ in the world?

The following chapters articulate various engagement methods at the intersection of the vertical depth and horizontal breadth of Christian life. Each offers a way to deepen and concretize individual and communal discernment. Each chapter begins with a story followed by a brief theological reflection and a practical parish application. Finally, reflection questions are given to help parish leaders consider the best next steps for initiating practices of deeper engagement.

Chapter Three

Where Have You Met God Lately?

A few parishioners from Spencer, West Virginia, told me about Sr. Barb during a picnic lunch welcoming me to the diocese. Sr. Barb was a Franciscan hermit nun who lived deep in a holler in the furthest reaches of the vicariate. She was rarely seen at meetings but always happy to receive visitors. Before I heard the word 'visitors,' I asked if I could meet her.

A few days later, I found myself driving in low gear down a steep series of hairpin turns on a one-lane dirt road, so steep I felt like my car was slowly falling hood first into a deep well. Following the long descent, I arrived at a thin strip of flat, fertile land next to a gentle babbling stream, a hidden refuge tucked into the folds of unforgiving mountains. I soon came upon a small wooden chapel next to the water and a log cabin set in the woods. Sr. Barb stood outside in rubber boots with a smile as large as the sun. As soon as I opened my car door, she greeted me. She was bubbly and energized yet surrounded by a calm and inviting patience.

She led me to her one-room hermitage nestled in the hill, where she spent her days weaving and praying. We sat on her small porch, listening to the birds welcome the day, and then she asked me, "Where have you met God lately?" This was the first question she asked me. I was not sure how to respond. No one had ever started a conversation with me in this way, certainly not a person I had just met. Nonetheless, I opened my mouth, and words began to flow out.

I was amazed at my own words. I told her about a God who had been present with me for as long as I could remember, how this God had called me consistently to service, and what I called the fullness of life. I also told her about the emptiness I often felt, even as people always reminded me of my best self. Barb was entirely focused on me. It was like my response was a great gift that she was receiving at that moment like I was Christmas to her. I felt heard and understood, free to express my inner experience without feeling judged or evaluated. It was a gift to be a gift. I finished speaking at some point, and with no more words, we both fell silent. She offered some words of insight but mostly gratefulness for my sharing. I felt I had been given a great gift even though I had done almost all the talking.

After some time, she stood up and invited me to walk. We slowly descended to the strawbale chapel, where we knelt in silent prayer before a tabernacle made of a simple carved and polished tree trunk. I shed tears for all that had emerged. Barb remained with me. The sound of the babbling water never stopped, just like the presence I had always known.

Theological Reflection - Divine Self-Communication

Fr. Karl Rahner, SJ, one of the great Catholic theologians of the 20th century and the primary architect of several of the documents of the Second Vatican Council, including *Dei Verbum* and *Lumen Gentium*, believed that God's deepest desire is for self-communication. God wants to communicate God's very self to us, and the essential nature of God is love. Rahner believed this communication was happening all around us and within us all the time and that humans have a unique ability to perceive this divine self-communication and respond in love to the love being expressed. God will stop at nothing and will employ every bit of creation to communicate. St. Ignatius of Loyola summarized this idea with his maxim, "God in all things." Ignatius also believed that God speaks in every event of our lives. He thought we could learn and grow into a closer union with God through prayerfully uncovering the divine in every facet of our lived experience.

The idea of divine self-communication, the immensity and urgency of the transmission, can also be understood through the horizontal and vertical intersection of the cross. God is inviting us into a vertical relationship through the Church's tradition, whose exact purpose is to transmit knowledge of God and mediate this relationship. In his Spiritual Exercises, St. Ignatius notes that "the Creator deals directly with the creature." In other words, God is addressing each human person directly before any mediating institution or tradition. Religion can shape the spiritual relationship between God and human beings but does not bring God. God is already in communication with each person.

God is also communicating through the horizontal experiences of our lives, our relationships with our families, friends, and fellow disciples, as well as the poor, disadvantaged, marginalized, victimized, and otherwise forgotten. God will use any opportunity, from the beauty of the created world to the cry of the poor, the wisdom of the ages and the play of children, tiny whispers and dramatic catastrophe, silence and song, laughter and tears. For those with ears to hear, all of these experiences can be encounters with the divine, with the God of self-communication who has been speaking since time began, who spoke through the prophets and still is, who guided the church through the Holy Spirit and still does, who revealed the way to restore our broken relationships and is still revealing.

Parish Application: Where have you encountered God?

This question immediately breaks through the flatness of experience, recognizing the divine is always present and accompanying us. The question presupposes that God is accessible, immediate, and recognizable. It immediately begins to create a new lens to evaluate one's experience relationally and intimately. The answer to this question is often, if not always, revelatory. It is an invitation to notice what is happening under the surface level. Through the answer, the individual articulates the image of the God they believe in and how God acts.

This question is not reserved for trained spiritual directors or clergy members. It is a question that anyone can ask, and everyone can answer without intricate theological language or concepts. It is an intimate question that invites vulnerability and an openness of trust and familiarity. When disciples ask this question of one another, they are moving to a deeper level together. They are sinking into vertical experience.

The question is a straightforward and open invitation. Still, several guidelines are critical to ensure no harm is done and a safe space is created for these tender conversations to unfold.

Gift-Giving

The question is not an invitation to debate. When someone shares with another person how they experience God in their lives, it is always a two-way gift. The listener is gifted by receiving the story, and the teller is blessed by hearing their story. The goal of the conversation is to listen and to share, not to judge, correct, compete or negate.

The listener is not expected to fix or answer the questions. It is tempting to give advice, especially when someone is seeking it. Often, people want to answer questions or address problems with easy fixes, but listeners are not experts and are not expected or encouraged to answer questions. Any definitive answer is usually inadequate as God and God's ways are mysterious and cannot be fully known. Therefore, humility is needed.

The answer is a gift. The response by the listener is simply gratitude and thanks for being gifted with the sacred story of another person. If there are complicated issues or the storyteller seeks help or resources, the listener should refer them to the parish's pastor or a trained spiritual director. Life can be very complicated, often painful and confusing. This is part of human life. We are not called upon to fix one another or offer simple answers to complex situations, but this should not prevent us from engaging one another. Faith communities are places where the truth of our lives can be shared, both our joys and broken pieces.

Begin with you

A pastor or member of the pastoral staff cannot ask parish members to do something they are not doing. It becomes a disingenuous exercise. Everyone in the parish is called to a relationship with the living God. Leaders are models and examples to everyone else. If you are a parish leader, who do you talk with about your experiences of God? Do you also ask this question of others? Answering the question is only half of the grace. The second half of the grace is in asking the question. Answering opens up a new lens, vocabulary, and way of talking and perceiving one's experience to see God as a living, accompanying force. Asking the question is equally as powerful. It requires that you create an open place to receive the sacred story of another. It invites you to be available, genuinely curious, and interested in what God is doing in another person's life. It is also an experience of being invited into another's sacred landscape.

Once you are comfortable asking and answering this question, you can request it from others. You might introduce it to the pastoral council or ministry team members. If there are prayer groups in the parish, such as a Rosary Altar Society, the finance council or any existing parish group invite them to share with a partner for the first 10 minutes of the meeting. Pastoral ministers model the ways of discipleship and then send others out to continue it. This exercise is a powerful means of empowerment. It gives parishioners an opening to grace that is immediately available and present. This practice of vertical inquiry deepens horizontal relationships within families, friends, and faith communities.

This question and the conversation are sacred. We are beginning to walk together more intentionally. We are asking about each other's graced experience. These tender, powerful stories often connect with profound disappointments, griefs, and wounds. The first time someone has the conversation, it might start on a fairly surface level, but as the inquiry winds further down, it touches our very core, our most profound sense of meaning, purpose, and value. We are inquiring about God, the center of one's meaning-making. It is not a conversation on the fly. It is not a question meant to be answered in 5 words. Parish leaders exercise ministry by creating the context and environment for this sacred encounter. The conversation can always be elaborated. What does that mean to you? What do you think God is trying to say to you? What does this say about who God is? The conversation ends with a prayer of thanksgiving for God's presence in our lives. It is not meant to be complicated, but it is meant to create depth and engagement.

As a parish progresses in spiritual engagement, gifts begin to emerge. People start noticing God everywhere, as St. Ignatius would say, "in all things." That is the point. We believe Christ is alive and living with us and among us if only we have eyes to see. This exercise and others like it equip disciples with eyes to recognize God working in their lives and encourage them to articulate it.

This question and others that invite a conversation on how God is present and working within our everyday experience can be a campaign within the parish. It can be asked at staff meetings, published in the bulletin, introduced in homilies, and encouraged within families. Responses to the question could also be gathered and posted so that the community begins to reflect together, notice, and learn how God is living and moving among them. The answers to this question reveal God's presence and shape with us. While the practice can become a consistent aspect of parish life, it could also be taken as a campaign during a liturgical season or in anticipation of a parish-wide communal discernment process. Either way, the goal is to empower everyone in the community to notice, name, and celebrate the presence of God in their midst.

Chapter Four

Breaking Open the Word

In March 2020, everything stopped. Covid changed all of our lives in a week. Global mass attendance plummeted. Many parishes began offering live stream masses, virtual catechesis, and RCIA via Zoom. Online offerings helped many Catholics stay connected, facilitating our social and faith connections. I was working at the Church of St. Francis Xavier in Manhattan. As a pastoral staff, we immediately began to shift and re-tool our program delivery. Our pastor installed a live camera system for streaming masses. The choir director moved rehearsals online, eventually creating blended recordings of individual choir members to offer virtual concerts.

To encourage the community during this unprecedented time of isolation, I began offering an open Zoom space on Saturday mornings for faith sharing around the weekly scripture. About 15 people appeared in the Zoom meeting room on that first morning, filled with anxiety and concern. The Zoom space provided a brief window of shared connection amid forced isolation. I invited everyone to offer prayer intentions for themselves,

others, and the world. The prayers came quickly cascading, one after the other, as we pleaded, 'Lord, hear our prayer' after each one. Many named friends, family members, and neighbors suffering from COVID-19, those in hospitals and nursing homes, medical personnel, first responders, and teachers. We brought the entire world into our Zoom room. With those intentions set in our minds and hearts, we read the scriptures we would hear again at mass on Sunday. Then, we shared our thoughts and reflections on the readings. Each person expressed what moved them in the readings and how it informed or applied to their life.

A committed group continued to meet each week throughout the pandemic. Eventually, people across the country joined our call as the virtual world existed beyond any geographic boundary. When the lockdown ended, I asked the group if they wanted to continue. They all did. Our Breaking Open the Word group meets weekly and always welcomes newcomers. We have become an ever-more connected and bonded community of faith. Together, we have come to recognize the signs and indicators of the Holy Spirit in our experience and name how we were being called to respond to the Gospel today.

Theological Reflection - The School of Communion

"Making the Church *the home and school of communion*: this is the great challenge that lies ahead of us in the millennium that is beginning if we want to be faithful to God's plan and also respond to the deepest expectations of the world."[4]

In 1999, at the dawn of the third millennium, St. Pope John Paul II published *Novo Millenio Inuente,* in which he defined communion as an ability to see our brothers and sisters in faith as "one who belongs to me."[5]

The local parish is the most immediate experience of this communion for most Catholics. The parish is a living expression of the sense of community we read about in the New Testament. We do not just tell the story of the living water. We are called to be a well where living water is found. When the Gospel is read in a faith community, parishioners should recognize their community as reflecting what they hear. The community embodies the story.

---

[4] Novo Millenio Inuente, 43.
[5] Ibid, 44.

Communion is not an abstract concept or a product to purchase but a way of being in a relationship that is immediately compelling and inviting. Those who gather around the Eucharistic table are missionaries of communion to one another.

At mass, can I say I am in communion with everyone else? How do I come to know their joys and sufferings? How am I being led into a deeper relationship with them? It is easy to be anonymous in a Catholic parish. Some have even called this an asset of the Catholic faith experience. You can go to mass, sit in the back, and no one will bother you. If Pope John Paul's call to communion is believed, this is not an asset but a cause for concern and growth.

When you look around at your faith community, are there people that you would call foreigners or strangers? Are they strangers to one another? If so, you have found your first goal. Parish communities are fertile ground for transformation simply by fostering a connection with the person in the next pew. The parish community is a gathering of strangers with a common faith. It is a challenge to break through the alienation, but in doing so, the stranger becomes part of you. The illusion of separation is pierced when we extend along the horizontal plane of faith.

Modern American culture mediates against relationships of communion. Twenty-five years after the publication of *Novo Millenio Inuente*, our society is more divided than ever. Polarization marks our politics and threatens to split families, communities, and the church. People are seen as commodities, burdens, inconveniences, or intruders. The individual is all that matters. We are encouraged to "look out for number 1" as life's primary task and goal. Our world alienates the stranger and fosters competition, exclusion, and hardness. Local faith communities are not idyllic neutral zones unaffected by polarization.

This makes the call to communion all the more relevant and challenging. Amid a culture of indifference and intolerance, Christian communities are called to a "revolution of tenderness"[6], intentional places of encounter where people are deliberately brought into connection. In this way, we become gifts to one another. We learn how to make room. The practice of "making

---

[6] Evangelii Gaudium, 88

room" creates an open space to allow another person's joys and sufferings to impact us. The surrounding culture encourages us to fill every empty space with products, distractions, self-interested endeavors, or accumulation. The Christian school of communion is an invitation to open a space within for others. Making room like this is also vertical and horizontal. When we make room for other people, we open space for God. We increase our capacity and foster empathy and compassion beyond the boundaries of family, faith, and existing belonging systems.

The work of communion begins with the person in the next pew. A great potential remains unrealized when we gather around the communion table but do not recognize the possible communion on our right and left. If cultivated, the community can grow together and become a more excellent reflection of God's presence in our midst.

Humans are relational and constituted for connections with others. Fostering communion, empathy, and interconnection is more about removing impediments to engagement than teaching a new skill. Impediments can stem from behaviors or beliefs adopted from contemporary society, learned protective mechanisms, or simply a lack of models and opportunities.

Creating opportunities for people to enter more deeply into generative communal relationships is the most basic and foundational exercise of an engaged parish. The opportunities emerge at that point of vertical and horizontal intersection. The goal is to draw out and deepen the vertical dimensions of one's relationship with God through an engagement with the horizontal. Since connection with the Spirit of God is innate and our very being relational, the opportunities for this deepening build upon our nature. The parish does not "teach" this skill as much as providing a space for it to flourish among people, giving it shape and connecting individual engagements to the larger community. The following application is a practical and easy-to-implement process to create a space for a deeper vertical and horizontal scripture engagement for any parish community.

Parish Application – Breaking Open the Word

Breaking Open the Word is a weekly lectionary-based spiritual conversation open to all parishioners. The format encourages full and active participation. Spiritual conversation lets each person articulate how God is active in their experience. At the same time, the format encourages active listening to others. This is an experience of "making room" for the sacred stories of others to enter and mingle with our own stories. In this mingling, the Spirit of the living God is present. Spiritual conversation is rooted in the promise of Christ, "When two or three are gathered, there I am in your midst."[7] The presence of Christ is not a memory but an active, living force residing at the core of all gathered. Spiritual conversation is an intentional space to name and engage the living Christ and allow God to inform and form His community through open and active listening.

The following steps can help parishes begin and sustain the practice of Breaking Open the Word.

---

[7] Matthew 18:20

Form a core group

A weekly scripture spiritual conversation starts with a core group of parishioners. Identify 5-7 initial participants based on gifts and interest. Initial participants may be selected, or they may self-select. In either case, providing a brief explanation of the practice will assist in the selection. The following is a brief explanation of Breaking Open the Word that can be used to invite core group members:

Breaking Open the Word is a shared reflection on the scripture of the week. Participants meet in small groups to read and reflect together on the scripture. This weekly conversation is a way to engage the word of God as a community, support one another, and pray together in a new way. A core group is now forming to learn and practice the process. Below are some gifts needed for this practice. If you feel called to reflect more deeply on God's word and want to share this experience with others, you are invited to join our first meeting.

Gifts needed include:

- *Openness and desire for spiritual growth*
- *Ease in working with groups*

- *Ability to listen to others without judgment*
- *Willingness to contribute to the spiritual growth of others*
- *Ability to commit to one hour a week for a designated period.*

Core group members should also have an interest or curiosity about the practice of spiritual conversation. Often, parishioners may possess some of these gifts and have an interest but are not known by parish leaders. Providing an open invitation with an overview of the practice and the initial commitment may elicit new participants who are curious.

It is important to invite people that have a degree of spiritual maturity. Spiritual conversation involves vulnerability and openness. Those who cannot tolerate difference or might be ideological, inflexible, or overly controlling would not be ideal candidates for the core group. The core group should be composed of individuals who are open to diverse points of view, can tolerate ambiguity, and do not bring a personal agenda to the process.

Core group members learn the method of spiritual conversation and begin the process together. As the process expands, core group members are invited to act as facilitators for other groups or virtual break-out groups. Experiencing and participating in the process is the best way to prepare to facilitate.

Learn together about Breaking Open the Word

The following concisely explains the underlying components and the Breaking Open the Word process. This information can be shared with the core group members in anticipation of the first session. A detailed outline of a session follows this explanation.

Breaking Open the Word is a spiritual conversation around the scriptures. The conversation involves active listening and speaking:

- *Active Listening* - All participants actively listen to the Scriptures, the Spirit in their midst, and the other group members. Active listening means that participants do not think about what they will say next but concentrate on what others say. This requires vulnerability and an openness to being affected by what others say. Active listening is welcoming, non-judgmental, and patient. It is a posture of presence and attention to the stirring of the Spirit in scripture and the experience of the other person sharing.

- *Intentional Speaking* means that each person is invited to offer a sincere expression of their experience. There are no spectators who only listen. Everyone in the spiritual conversation is invited to speak and share from the heart of their own experience. Speaking from experience is a generous offering to others. It is a gift. When brought together in the context of prayer, active listening and intentional speaking can be experiences of conversion, reconciliation, and even transformation as participants enter more deeply into scriptures and learn to listen more deeply to the experience of others.

Setting

- **In-person** – If held in person, the session occurs in a comfortable room with chairs set in a circle. The ideal group size is six, ranging from 5-7. A low table is set in the center of the circle. The table is set with a prayer space, including a cloth of the liturgical color, a bible, a candle, and perhaps a plant or flower. Try to minimize distractions as much as possible. As the groups expand, additional circles can be created. Ideally, these additional circles are arranged in other spaces free from distraction. Each group requires a facilitator.

- **Virtual** - Breaking Open the Word works well in a virtual environment and may be more convenient for many people. In a virtual environment, the opening section, which includes scripture reading, occurs in a main Zoom room. Then, if necessary, participants are placed in break-out rooms of 5-7 people. A facilitator is required for each break-out room.

Process

The steps of a Breaking Open the Word session are as follows:

- **Welcome** – The facilitator welcomes everyone to the session and invites everyone to sit. When all are ready, the session begins.

- **Silence** - Breaking the Word begins in silence. A time of silence welcomes God into our midst. Silence allows busy minds to settle, leaving behind any hectic commotion of the day. It focuses and allows everyone to arrive.

- **Opening Prayer** - A brief opening prayer invites the Holy Spirit to be present and speak to us through scripture and the experiences that will be shared.

- **Intentions** – All participants are invited to name any prayer intentions they want to offer. Mutuality, vulnerability, and openness are cultivated as participants share their concerns and ask for God's intervention and presence in the world. Prayers are spontaneous. Not all participants may articulate an intention. Some may have more than one intention. Sufficient time is given to name all intentions. All participants are invited to intone "Lord, hear our prayer" after each intention, modeling the prayers of the faithful.

- **Preparation Song** – A preparatory song can be played before the scriptures are read. The song is brief but helps all participants to focus and prepare to listen deeply. A gospel acclamation from the liturgical season works well. Our initial group uses a gospel acclamation recorded by the Monks of the Weston Priory called Welcome to the Gospel on their album "Hear the Song of Your People."

- **Reading of Scripture** – Normally, the first and second readings are read as well as the Gospel. Before the meeting, the facilitator should select people to read each. A brief pause occurs between each reading. *(If the readings are very long, such as* *the Emmaus story, the Man Born Blind, or the Raising of Lazarus, etc., there is an option to only read the Gospel)* If done in person, the facilitator moves on to the first movement after a brief pause. If the session is virtual, participants are placed in break-out rooms after reading the Gospel. Break out group facilitators, then introduce the first movement.

- **First Movement** – The facilitator invites participants to articulate any words, phrases, or ideas that stood out to them as they listened to the readings and explain why. In this first round, participants connect their own life experiences to the words of scripture and vice versa. **There is no cross-talk or dialogue.** Each person is invited to speak freely without interruption. Everyone else in the small group actively listens to the one speaking. No time limit is given. The facilitator also participates but should not be the first one to speak. Participants can take notes on any ideas resonating with them as they listen. These notes may be helpful in the second movement.

- **Silence** - Once everyone has spoken, a minute of silence is observed. This allows all articulated thoughts to settle and for the Spirit to be present.

- **Second Movement** - The facilitator invites participants to comment on anything that resonated with them as they listened to the other participants. This second round encourages participants to connect to what others have shared. It is not a time for giving advice or refuting what others have said but to name any grace, connection, or insights emerging from their listening.

- **Silence** - Once everyone has spoken, a minute of silence is observed. This allows all articulated thoughts to settle and for the Spirit to be present.

- **Third Movement** – The facilitator invites participants to offer a summary by giving a title or name to the conversation they have just had or to articulate the grace of the experience. This last moment, while brief, is a reflection on the reflection. It is often the moment when the presence of the Spirit is most pronounced and the lessons or takeaways most clearly articulated.

- **Closing Prayer** – If the session is held virtually, participants return to the main room after completing the third movement. Then, the primary facilitator or someone delegated offers a final prayer of thanks for the presence of the Spirit in the group.

Outline

The outline for Breaking Open the Word is as follows:

1. Welcome and Gathering
2. Opening Prayer
3. Prayer Intentions (Response: Lord, hear our prayer)
4. Focusing Song
5. Reading of Scripture (1st and 2nd Reading and Gospel)

6. *(Move to Break-out rooms if virtual)*

7. First movement (What stood out to you and why)

8. Silence – one minute

9. Second movement (What stood out to you as you listened to others and why)

10. Silence – one minute

11. Third movement (What would you title our conversation, or what are the graces of our time together)

12. *(Virtual break-out groups return to large group)*

13. Large-Group Closing Prayer

Spreading the Net – Expanding the Conversation

As the core group learns the process, they facilitate additional sessions. The core group members encourage more participants by sharing their experiences. One of the most effective methods of encouragement is personal witness. Core group members can be invited to speak briefly to the congregation at the end of mass to describe their experience and invite others to participate.

When expanding the group, a registration process is encouraged. Pre-registration can help determine the number of facilitators needed, the number of rooms and chairs required (if done in-person), and the number of break-out rooms (if virtual).

Once the process takes root within the parish, it becomes self-sustaining. As long as there are sufficient facilitators for the small groups and ongoing invitations, the groups can operate every week without a great deal of intervention.

It is recommended that facilitators meet together twice a year to reflect on their experience, name the graces they have witnessed, and address any concerns that have arisen. These are opportunities to evaluate the initiative, handle logistical or programmatic adjustments, and offer ongoing support and appreciation for the facilitators.

Breaking Open the Word allows Catholics to deepen their reception of the Gospel while building community. The entire faith community, from the pastor to catechists, lectors, altar servers, parish elders, and neophytes, can all grow closer to one another, break through the illusion of separateness, and experience the living Christ at the heart of their community through this simple and powerful experience of God's word.

Chapter Five

Parish Pastoral Councils

The Agent of Communal Discernment

When I first arrived in the Diocese of Brooklyn, I went on a parish-wide tour to meet with pastors and discuss their hopes and anxieties around the pastoral planning initiative mandated by the Bishop. It was not an easy sell. Many pastors had lived through many "Disneyland rides," yearly panacea programs that consistently emerged from the diocese to revolutionize parish life. Brooklyn had piloted and promoted many parish programs in the past, and they all seemed to follow a predictable pattern of hype, work, partial engagement, and then a waning of energy and eventual demise. About half of the pastors were genuinely interested and even raved about a comprehensive pastoral planning process that promised deep and sustained engagement. This also meant that half of the pastors were very suspicious of the initiative, unsure that it would have desirable effects or endure for more than the startup phase, providing them with yet another binder to put on their shelves.

Fr. Dennis Farrell was in this latter camp, but he did invite me to dinner at the rectory, and I always accepted such an invitation. Dinner at the rectory was a time to hear what was happening in the diocese and share in fellowship with the pastor and the priests. Rectory dinners usually followed a standard format. All sat around a large dining room table. The pastor was at the head of the table, followed by other priests living at the parish. The principal of the school or the DRE would often join. As a special guest, I was seated by the pastor. High school students, usually girls, would serve the food, bringing out dishes from the kitchen. A bell on the table was rung when the course was finished, and the students would enter to clear the plates and bring in dessert. There was always dessert.

Fr. Farrell had been cordial and welcoming. He was a great supporter of the Boy Scouts, so we swapped summer camp stories. When the plates were cleared, and before dessert and coffee came out, he turned the screw. In his dry tone, he asked, "Parish Councils, didn't they die years ago?" Brilliant. In just a few words, he attempted to cut me off at the knees, labeling my mandate as outdated and irrelevant, a relic from the dustbin of church history. I countered immediately, "Well, Father, you know this religion. It is all about resurrection." He was amused but not convinced. I knew rattling off my talking points on the benefits of planning, consultation, and parishioner engagement would not impress him, so I asked him why he believed councils died. He lamented the overly politicized parish councils of the 1980s. They created cliques. The members felt they could challenge the pastor on every matter of policy. They brought a democratic mindset and thought a majority vote would negate his decision-making ability. And finally, no one in the parish even knew who the council members were, yet they were infused with an overblown sense of self-importance.

I asked Fr. Farrell to give me one chance. Could we work together to create a selection process for new council members that would not be political? I offered to facilitate a community discernment involving all parishioners that would result in the selection of lay leaders with the gifts needed and a service mindset. He assured me an election would never work. I told him I was not offering an election but a way of selecting to model inclusion and transparency. Members would be chosen based on gifts, and the entire process would be rooted in the parish's mission. Surprisingly, he agreed, more curious than convinced, but that was enough.

Over the next six weeks, I assisted Fr. Farrell in the selection process for new pastoral council members, which is articulated in this chapter. In the end, Holy Name Parish chose 12 new council members. Some were well-known pillars of the community. Some were newcomers to the parish. All were clear on the role of the Parish Pastoral Council, aware of the gifts they possessed and ready to be of service. They were also all affirmed and confirmed by the entire parish and the pastor. When evaluating the process, Fr. Farrell finally admitted that the past dead councils were nothing like this group. He now had a committed group of talented parishioners looking at the parish with the same lens. They were enthusiastic and open. They were not coming in with an ax to grind or a private agenda to fulfill. They were committed to working towards the enhancement and development of their parish and to doing the work to make it happen.

Theological Background - Communal Discernment

Thus far, the focus has been on interpersonal and individual forms of discernment. Discernment is a critical task in the spiritual life as each baptized Christian has a personal relationship with God and is called to use their gifts to live out the Christian mission in a unique way. The task of discernment is a life-long endeavor that deepens as one's relationship with Christ grows. The vertical line extends further, and the horizontal dimension of relationships, family, work, community, and parish grows deeper. The engagement processes already described are meant to assist individuals in naming the movement and presence of God in their lives and the world around them.

Christian communities are environments where individuals can join others on a similar journey to learn about God, grow together, support one another, suffer and rejoice, and encourage and celebrate. We help each other on this journey.

But discernment does not end there. Parish communities are also in a collective relationship with Christ, called to live out the mission Christ has entrusted. Each Catholic parish is called to be the presence of the living Christ in their particular location. St. Theresa of Avila perhaps said it best, "Christ has no other hands on Earth now but yours." Parish communities are constituted to be the hands and feet of Christ where they are. To do this effectively and faithfully, the community must discern how God is calling them to live out the Gospel in light of their situation, culture, and time.

While the Church has a mission rooted in the Gospel instituted by Christ and remains consistent throughout time, the way this mission is lived out in each particular place will be unique. Christ is alive and dynamic in the lives of each Christian and the life of each community. Communal discernment is the deliberate act of engaging the living Christ, the Spirit present in each community. Through communal discernment, the parish community discovers how they are being invited and encouraged to respond to the call of the Gospel now.

How does the Christian community discern the will of Christ together? The methods and processes used reveal what a community believes. In the past, the pastor made most decisions regarding a parish's future direction and priorities. The pastor may or may not have consulted or listened to others. That was his prerogative, but the community's discernment was ultimately left to one faithful member. This process revealed what was believed. The Spirit of God was discernable by the clergy, empowered through Holy Orders. The participation of the rest of the faithful was not required to discern the will of God. This methodology was congruent with the theological understanding of the pre-Vatican church that rooted the call to ministry and holiness in the sacrament of Holy Orders.

The renewed theology of Vatican II grounds the call to holiness and ministry in baptism, recognizing that all the baptized participate in the mission of Christ and all are called to holiness. Such a dramatic shift in theological understanding also requires a change in methodology. If all are called to holiness and Christ is alive and present to every member of the community, then a true and complete discernment of the will of Christ for the community would require the participation and input of every member. Such a broad level of participation and inclusion can reveal an incredible buried treasure that has always been present in the living Church. Suppose the Spirit of God is in communication and relationship with each baptized Catholic, calling them to holiness, community, and mission. In that case, their input and participation in the spiritual process of discerning the will of God for the community can provide rich insights and depth that have been missing or absent in previous eras.

Each member holds something valuable, both gifts and insight, to build up the Body of Christ. St. Paul teaches that there are many parts to the body, and each part of the body serves a purpose for the whole, but each part also offers a unique and valuable perspective.[8] The view of the foot differs from the head and from the eye. The perspective of the most vulnerable differs from that of the strongest and most exposed. All are valuable and necessary to understanding the body's totality and Christ's understanding. Inviting the participation of all in the discernment of the whole can bring greater clarity, understanding, and a stronger connection to the body.

Unfortunately, full participation of all members in communal discernment has not occurred in many parishes. In these cases, there is the danger of an incongruence between the theological understanding of the Church and the practice of the local communities.

---

[8] 1 Cor. 12:12

Some incongruence was inevitable. The documents of Vatican II present an aspirational vision of the Church. Time, effort, and deliberate change were required for local parish communities to embody this theological understanding. Over the past 60 years, bishops and pastors have engaged the laity in many creative and innovative ways to encourage wider participation and collaboration. The faithful's full involvement in communal discernment processes can develop much further. While broad participation will always be more labor-intensive and time-consuming than unilateral decision-making, it is more authentic to the apostolic tradition. It has the potential to revitalize and engage parishioners in new and dynamic ways that deepen their relationship with one another, the parish, and their faith.

The Vatican Council provided nascent structures for bishops and pastors to develop the inclusion of the laity in communal discernment. The Parish Pastoral Council is the primary body offered in the Vatican documents and later in the revised Canon Law.

Parish Councils were first mentioned in the Vatican II "Decree on the Apostolate of the Laity." In that document, the council fathers said:

In Dioceses, as far as possible, councils should be set up to assist the Church's apostolic work, whether in the field of evangelization and sanctification or in the fields of charity, social relations and the rest. Such councils should be found too, if possible, at parochial, inter-diocesan level and also on the national and international place.[9]

Initially, the bishops at the Council were first proposing Diocesan Pastoral Councils when they called for the creation of councils, and only secondly, and "if possible," were they considered on the parish level. Yet, over the past 60 years, diocesan and parish pastoral councils have flourished and sometimes floundered even as their exact purpose, nature, composition, and aim have continued to be debated. The Council proposed but did not define all aspects. The document calls for councils, points to a few focus subjects, and leaves the implementation to future generations. The 1983 Code of Canon Law does not go much further. Canon 536 leaves the development of

---

[9] Decree on the Apostolate of the Laity, 23.

councils to the discretion of the local bishop and encourages them to "foster pastoral activity."[10]

Pope Francis referred to councils early in his pontificate as he announced, "How necessary are parish councils! How could a pastor run a parish without a pastoral council?" He called these councils "organs of communion."[11] connecting their role to the essential process of listening and discerning God's will for the Church's life. It is in this sense that councils undertake their consultative ministry.

As a consultative body, the parish pastoral council collaborates with the pastor to exercise continual discernment. Council members are leaders in the parish exercising a vital service. They serve the larger community by creating environments for listening, receiving, and considering the "sensus fidelium," the sense of the faithful. Lumen Gentium 12 teaches that when the faithful discern together, they can perceive God's true will. Authentic discernment, located at the intersection of the vertical and horizontal, seeks to understand the will of the living God for the church in the unique time and place

---

[10] Canon 536 §1
[11] Pope Francis, "Address to clergy of Assisi", Oct. 4, 2013

where the faithful exist. Parish Pastoral Councils work collaboratively with their pastor to provide a process of communal discernment that invites all parishioners to contribute to a shared plan to live out the Gospel mission in their local place.

Service on the Parish Pastoral Council is a significant moment in discipleship as members are called to offer their gifts to serve the community. Council membership is often understood as having a privileged voice that the pastor listens to more closely than others. It can be seen as a position of preferential influence. True service on the parish pastoral council is just the opposite. As servant leaders, council members create spaces where others can have their voices heard, listen to others, and work collaboratively to discern God's will. Parish Pastoral Councils offer a listening space that grounds decision-making.

The council has a balcony view of the parish focused on the overall well-being and engagement of the entire community. This requires learning about the community as a whole through listening and study. This ministry requires data collection and presentation to share the state of the community's life and its growing edges with others. Acquiring this wide-angle lens requires putting aside agendas to be attentive to the needs of all, especially the most vulnerable and excluded.

Before beginning communal discernment, it may be necessary to determine if the council is prepared and able to act as the agents of communal discernment. Do the council members understand themselves as servant leaders? Do they know their role as consultative and facilitators of consultative processes? Is the council visionary or functionary? Do members focus on their interests or only one group, or are they concerned for the entire parish? Do members regularly rotate on and off the council, or have the same members been there for more than 5, 10, or 20 years? Having the right people with the right gifts and understanding on the council is critical to authentic discernment. New council members may need to be discerned. Other members may need to cycle off the council. Staggering term limits may need to be established along with a process of selection that includes community input.

Parish Application

Discernment of New Parish Pastoral Council Members

How we do anything reveals our beliefs about everything. Practice demonstrates more clearly than words what a community believes about itself and how God is present in the community. A pastor can espouse spiritual discernment, servant leadership, and full participation. Still, the disconnect is easily perceived if actual practices foster exclusion and cliques or are rooted in a person-driven agenda. What matters is what happens.

Selecting parish pastoral council members can lay the groundwork for communal discernment. The way that council members are chosen communicates the nature of the ministry. It is incongruent to announce the creation or reconstitution of a leadership body responsible for facilitating a parish-wide discernment and then not use principles of discernment to select those leaders. Communal discernment is undermined when a popular election or simple appointment is used to choose the leaders. The selection process can model the experience of full participation, gift discernment, prayer, and listening.

The selection process is an opportunity to demonstrate what will ground and drive all that follows.

The following application is rooted in the principles and values of communal discernment. It is designed to offer an initial experience of communal discernment. This selection process is grounded and driven by the following:

- Participation of the entire faith community in the selection process
- Educating the whole parish about the mission of the parish and the role of the council
- A process focused on the gifts of individuals, not on visibility or popularity
- The use of prayer, faith-sharing, active listening, and consensus-building
- A method for eliciting potential leaders within the parish
- Affirms all nominees and minimizes the sense of winner/loser
- An open and transparent process
- An engagement of everyone who is nominated

The discernment process for selecting new members of a Parish Pastoral Council members can be completed in about eight weeks. The process steps are below, and a checklist of activities for each step follows.

Publicity (1-3 weeks before nomination)

Parish Discernment and the Parish Pastoral Council (PPC) are explained throughout the parish over several weeks. This is a time of invitation and parish-wide education on the parish's mission and the call to participation. This might include:

- Pulpit announcements by pastor and/or existing council members introducing the open nomination process and an invitation to participate
- Bulletin announcements. Several samples are included
- Posters, flyers, homily references, prayer cards, or general intercessions

The publicity introduces communal discernment to the larger community. Connecting the nomination of council members to the larger initiative of discerning the parish's future may help frame the publicity.

Publicity clarifies the role of the Parish Pastoral Council as a visionary planning group. Council members are selected based on their gifts for visioning, planning, and leadership. They are not chosen based on position, title, tenure, or other reasons. A list of qualities for a parish pastoral council member is included on the nomination form and can be used in publicity materials.

Nominations (Week 4)

At all masses on one weekend, nomination forms are distributed or left in the pews along with pencils or pens. Parishioners are encouraged to write the names of individuals who they believe have gifts for leadership. The pastor or an existing council member explains the nomination process at the end of the homily or after communion. During this explanation, parishioners are made aware that nominees will be contacted and invited to consider being a candidate. Parishioners are encouraged to nominate fellow parishioners, but self-nomination is also accepted. Ushers collect the forms during the collection or after communion.

Alternatively, the same nomination form can be posted on the parish website. A QR code can be created to link to the form. The QR code can be printed in the bulletin or posted in the pew. Parishioners can use their phones to open the QR Code and complete their nomination form.

Invitations (Week 5)

Invitations are sent out to nominees as soon as possible after the nominations have been collected. The invitation is first an acknowledgment of the gifts of the individual. Someone in the parish nominated them because they believed the candidate has the gifts needed for leadership. This should be recognized. Second, the invitation indicates the date and time of the Information Session. Nominees are invited to attend the Information Session to learn about the ministry they are asked to consider. There is no obligation or commitment at this time. It is only an invitation to come and learn more.

In addition, formal invitations allow the pastor, if necessary, to remove any names based on his pastoral insight. However, nominations should be removed with great discretion to maintain the integrity of the process.

The Information night is usually scheduled one week (or two weeks at the most) after the Nomination Weekend.

Information Session (Week 6)

This presentation is a time for nominees to learn about the Parish Pastoral Council and ask questions regarding this ministry. It consists of:

- Faith-sharing
- A presentation on the basics of parish pastoral councils and communal discernment
- Time for the pastor to express his hope and vision for the Parish Pastoral Council
- Logistical details - including the frequency and number of meetings and the needed commitment for the formation process

The Information Session is held at the parish and usually lasts 1 hour. Most dioceses have resources regarding parish councils and often have speakers available.

Evening of Discernment (Week 7)

The Night of Discernment is held one week after the Information Session. Because this process seeks to narrow the number of nominees, those who could not attend the Information Session are usually not allowed to attend the Night of Discernment.

The evening includes a period of prayer and listening, followed by a group-wide consensus process in which participants become selectors, affirming those individuals whose gifts are needed at this time on the council. The candidates who emerge from the consensus process become the new Parish Pastoral Council Members. A program and explanation of this discernment process is included in Appendix I. The worship aid for the process is found in Appendix II.

Commissioning of New Members (Week 8)

The pastor commissions the new members the weekend after the Night of Discernment. This commissioning could also be a time to recognize those leaving the existing council or to recognize anyone who assisted in the selection process. A sample commissioning service is included in Appendix V.

Chapter Six
A One-to-One Conversation Campaign
Discerning the Future of the Parish with Individuals

"So, is this something like Catholic speed dating?" A few trepidatious parishioners entered the parish hall after mass at this large urban church in the shadow of the Verrazano Bridge in Brooklyn's Dyker Heights neighborhood. The regular tables were in the center of the gym, where parishioners were used to coming each Sunday for coffee and cookies following mass, but this week was a bit different. The Parish Pastoral Council had announced they would be available for individual conversations with parishioners to hear their concerns and hopes for the parish and neighborhood. Chairs were set in pairs around the hall. In each pair, one chair was empty. In the other, a council member sat ready to listen.

With some hesitation, parishioners poured their coffee as the council members invited them to sit for a short chat. A few people sat down, and others soon saw that the conversations were easy and engaging. Soon, every chair was filled, and conversation filled the room. A chair would empty every few minutes and someone else would take their turn. Council members listened, took notes, and thanked parishioners for their input. Parishioners thanked the council members, too, commenting that this was the first time someone had asked them for their thoughts on the parish's future. The council members assured them that this would not be the last.

Theological Reflection – Empowered by Baptism

Through listening and consultation, parish pastoral councils undertake a vital task of co-responsibility with the pastor in gathering and interpreting the joys and hopes, the griefs and concerns of the wider community. The council is at the service of the community. The council also provides an inclusive space for prayerful discernment, demonstrating that every voice matters.

The practice of consultation is grounded in baptism. Baptism is a sacramental moment of incorporation into the People of God. As members of the People of God, each baptized Catholic "shares a true equality with regard to the dignity and the activity common to all the Faithful for the building up of the Body of Christ."[12] Every baptized person plays a role in the building up of the kingdom and are called to the "priestly, prophetic and kingly functions of Christ"[13] Part of this function is lived out through consultation. Lumen Gentium boldly claims that "the totality of the Faithful cannot err in matters of belief...when they show universal agreement in matters of faith and morals."[14] Sincere inquiry into the ideas and insights of the local community of the faithful is a genuine pursuit of the Spirit who guides the faithful "to all truth."[15] This is the goal of all listening processes, consultation, and communal discernment.

Pope Francis has said that the faithful have "an instinct for discerning the way that God is calling the Church"[16] Consultation rests on the belief that the Spirit is alive in the faith community and that the baptized faithful can discern the will of the Spirit together. This occurs "through the contemplation and study of believers who

---

[12] Lumen Gentium, 32.
[13] Code of Canon Law, 204.
[14] Lumen Gentium, 12.
[15] John 16:13.
[16] Francis, "On the 50th Anniversary of the Synod of Bishops," Oct. 17, 2015.

78

treasure these things in their hearts."[17] Pastors are called to be the "authentic guardians, interpreters, and witnesses of the faith of the whole Church."[18] This establishes a dynamic relationship of listening, responding, discerning, and co-responsibility "in accord with the condition proper to each."[19] In other words, the clergy and the laity are both called to participate in the discernment of the Spirit, and each has a responsibility. The faithful are called to participate by sharing their insights, ideas, and perspectives. Pastors are called to listen, discern, name the way, and lead the community in the path of the Spirit's will.

Parish Application – One-to-One Listening Campaign

The pastor and pastoral council can employ various consultation methods to ascertain the "sensus fidei" or sense of the faithful. Consultations can occur in large assemblies, in smaller focus groups, or even through

---

[17] Dei Verbum, 8.
[18] Francis, "On the 50th Anniversary of the Synod of Bishops," Oct. 17, 2015.
[19] Code of Canon Law, 204.

surveys and questionnaires. Each method has its advantages and challenges.

A one-to-one listening campaign is an ideal consultative method to begin a communal discernment process. This form of consultation consists of individual meetings to listen to the experiences and insights of one other person. This type of listening process is subjective. The responses are personalized, yet the conversation focuses on the life and future of the parish community. A structured campaign of individual conversations yields many results that foster life and engagement within the parish. The conversations are opportunities to build and deepen relationships in the parish, get a sense of individual parishioners' concerns and hopes, and gain critical insight into how others view the parish. The consultation reveals strengths, areas of needed growth, and how the broader community perceives the parish. Other consultative methods engage groups of people, consider scripture and objective data, or reflect on the parish's mission. One-to-one conversations focus on the experience and perspective of individuals, gauge their interest, hope, concerns, and enthusiasm, and then invite them to more involvement in the discernment process by attending future consultations with other parishioners.

Every faith community's challenge and goal is building relationships among individual members. Creating opportunities for interpersonal connection is integral to the parish's mission. Cultivating connections builds up the Body of Christ. One-to-one conversations are designed to provide the pastor and council input as part of a communal discernment process. Still, they also help to make connections and encourage greater participation of parish members, many of whom have never been asked about their views and insights about their community. These connections will become a strength when it is time to implement new initiatives in the parish. The first step, though, is incorporating and including people through listening, demonstrating that each individual matters and is vital to the community's life.

Another goal and advantage of a one-to-one consultation campaign is identifying gifts, hopes, and enthusiasm. St. Paul says, "To each individual, the manifestation of the Spirit is given for some benefit."[20] An

---

[20] 1 Cor 12:7.

individual conversation can help identify the gifts that the individual might possess and how the Spirit manifests in them for the benefit of others. Therefore, one goal of the conversation is to ascertain the individual's potential for leadership, their gifts, and what interests and excites them about their faith and the parish.

One-to-one conversations occur as a campaign. It is a discernment methodology employed to determine how the Holy Spirit is calling the community to move forward into the future. The conversations are not ongoing or random. They have a focus and a duration. The campaign is launched for some time and then concludes. The conclusion is tied to the discernment process, usually leading to a culminating consultation such as an assembly or series of focus groups where parishioners can discuss where they believe the Spirit is calling them.

What is a one-to-one conversation, and what is it not?

The goal of a one-to-one conversation campaign as part of a parish consultation is to discern the will of God for the parish. This makes these conversations different than other types of conversations. First, while the conversations only involve two people, they are public conversations. The conversations focus on the individual's ideas about the parish. Conversations are not psychological or therapeutic. Council members are not listening to fix, change, or cure anyone of anything or to diagnose the individual.

Also, listening is not undertaken as a customer survey designed to improve products, programs, or procedures. Parishioners are not clients. Instead, each parish member is working collaboratively with the pastor and the council to understand the call of God and the way the parish can live the Gospel mission more faithfully.

Lastly, this listening is not like political canvasing in which the listener attempts to ascertain the individual's self-interest, political affiliation, or public policy desire. The listening is focused on how the individual believes God is calling the community now to respond to the deepest needs of the parish, the neighborhood, and the world as the Gospel demands.

One-to-One

One-to-one conversations only involve two people. It is one person talking to one person. It is not meant to be a group interview with two council members talking to one person or one council member talking with two parishioners. This is true even with married couples. The conversation provides an opportunity for a single individual to express their thoughts and feelings about the parish in a confidential environment, but also with the knowledge that their insights will be considered part of the larger parish discernment process.

Focused

The conversations are focused on the parish, its mission and activities, and hopes for the future. There is a time for introductions and breaking the ice, but the conversation is not chit-chat. It is important to respect the time the other person is offering and keep to the point of the conversation.

Planned

The conversation is planned. It is scheduled for a specific time and only for this purpose. It is not a conversation on the fly, on the way out of church, or a random meeting on the street. The conversation is scheduled for a period of time and should not be open-ended. The meeting has a beginning and an ending time, which should also be respected. The sessions last between 20-30 minutes, but no more.

Parts of the Conversation

The conversation follows a specified format. The steps are as follows:

Opening Credential

The council members begin by introducing themselves and credentialing as part of the parish council or the leadership planning team. This establishes that they have credibility and speak to you as part of a parish discernment process.

Breaking the Ice

Breaking the Ice is a simple but important step that involves offering some information about yourself, which leads to an opening for the person to share something about themselves. For instance, "I have been a parishioner here at St. Joseph's for 23 years. It has been a wonderful spiritual home for my family and me. How did you first come to St. Joseph?"

Learning about the other person

The majority of the conversation is focused on learning about the other person. The learning involves their ideas about the parish, their hopes and concerns, and how they feel the parish could grow and be more effective. In addition, ask about the person's interests, passions, and gifts. You are learning about their ideas, potential, and interest in contributing to the life of the parish.

Closing/Next Steps

In closing, thank the individual for their time and participation. Assure them that their input will be shared with the broader planning group and the pastor and will be part of the more extensive discernment process of the parish. Invite them to continue participating in the next steps of the discernment process (assembly, focus groups, etc.)

Beginning a Conversation Campaign

Council members may initially be a bit apprehensive when organizing a one-to-one campaign. It takes a few conversations to feel comfortable and confident. Therefore, it begins with council members having conversations with one another. Divide into two groups, starting with one person acting as the council member and the other as the participant. After ten minutes, switch roles and begin again. Debrief these experiences with one another.

When organizing a conversation campaign, encourage council members to begin with people they know and feel comfortable with before moving out to meet with parishioners they have not met yet. The process becomes more comfortable and engaging once council members have had a few good conversations. Typically, council members are very energized by these conversations.

Committing to Conversations

When organizing a conversation campaign, each council member should commit to having a certain number of conversations over a period of time. The number that each person commits to should be based on what they can reasonably accomplish. They should set the number themselves. Council members may select a different number based on their circumstances. Someone with a full-time job and a young family may only be able to schedule one or two weekly meetings. In comparison, a retired person may have more free time and could schedule more meetings. In any case, each person should commit to completing several conversations, and the total number becomes the campaign's goal.

Notes and Reporting

Council members record a few notes from the conversation directly after the conversation. They do not take notes during the conversation but remain attentive and focused on the person. However, as soon as it is finished, the council members should write down every important point they remember. A shared Google Doc could be created where each council member could add notes, and everyone else could immediately see them.

Debriefing and Reporting Back

After the campaign, the council meets to debrief the overall experience and reflect on the notes and content of the conversations. This discerning conversation focuses on significant themes repeated by participants, insights gained, and surprises or people they met. As part of this meeting, council members consider any parish group not represented in the campaign. Where all ages, cultural, and language groups included? Is there any unrepresented group that still needs to be invited?

From this debriefing conversation, salient themes, emerging consensus points, and creative ideas are compiled into a brief report to the parish. The pastor or a council member reports to the larger parish on the campaign results. The report includes the number of meetings held and the emerging salient points. This report concludes with an invitation for all parishioners to participate in the next steps of the discernment process (usually a parish assembly or focus groups). One-to-one conversations are generally used to begin a discernment process, leading to a next engagement step where parishioners are invited to discern together. The one-to-one conversations provide a forum for individual reflection. The next step is discernment in common.

Chapter Seven

Parish Survey:

Engaging the Signs of the Times

The Diocese of Brooklyn is the smallest geographic Roman Catholic diocese in the United States but the fifth largest diocese in population. It is also one of only two dioceses in the world that is part of a larger city. The Diocese of Brooklyn comprises two boroughs of New York City: Brooklyn and Queens. The total area is about 76 square miles, with a Catholic population of 1.2 million out of a population approaching 3.5 million. When I joined the Pastoral Planning Office in 2005, a primary task of the office was developing a demographic study of each of the 220 parishes within the diocese to assist pastors and parish leaders as they developed relevant plans to advance the mission of the Gospel. These data reports would become a mirror that the faith community could look at as they considered their position within their broader neighborhood and their internal challenges and strengths as they considered their future.

Our office's initiative became the largest census the diocese had ever undertaken. Our goal was simple.

Accomplishing it was anything but. We wanted to survey every mass-attending Catholic on a single weekend to capture a snapshot of the diocese and each parish. Then, we wanted to compare the data from each parish with the census data from the broader neighborhood where the parish was located. In this way, we could generate a report for each parish revealing who they were and who was around them. Finally, we would pose mission-focused questions around outreach and evangelization to help them consider the data.

This task was enormous, and it was also 2005. This was before the dawn of the smartphone. I was still using a road atlas. GPS was only an idea. QR codes did not exist. Most parishes in the diocese still used fax machines to share documents. Yet, our charge was clear. We developed a questionnaire that exactly matched 15 questions from the US Census. This included information on age, race, gender, length of residency, household income, and the like. We created a paper Scantron form in 6 different languages: English, Spanish, Polish, Creole, Korean, and Chinese. We then sent forms to every parish, one for each parishioner.

Then, during all masses on a single weekend, every parish distributed the forms along with golf pencils, had everyone complete them, and handed them back to the ushers. While we did receive pushback from several pastors regarding the interruption that this survey-taking would create in the middle of the liturgy, we stressed that this exercise was a critical task for the community, a collective participation in the missionary exercise of communal discernment. Therefore, the liturgy, the central moment of the community's life, was where such an exercise should be undertaken.

The following Monday, boxes of paper started pouring in from every direction. In the end, we collected over 180,000 pieces of paper. These forms became the basis of parish, deanery, vicariate, and diocesan reports that showed the parish survey results next to the same information from the US census blocks comprising the parish boundaries. In many cases, the mirror that we created was stunning, challenging, and even uncomfortable for some. It revealed wealthy parishes in impoverished neighborhoods, elderly communities in neighborhoods filled with young professionals, African-American communities in rapidly gentrifying neighborhoods, and entire census tracks of new residents surrounding a struggling community of longtime residents.

The parish survey reflected the complexity and rapid social changes affecting the parishes and the neighborhoods in which they were called to be the presence of Christ for all.   The parish survey became a wake-up call for many. It was a chance to see who we were and how the world was changing. When the parish members and leaders came together to discuss their future and their priorities, the mirror of the parish survey became an objective lens that helped every parishioner take a wide view of who they were and where they were as they decided together where the Spirit of God was asking them to go.

Theological Reflection – Signs of the Times

A primary step in any communal discernment process is reading the "Sign of the Times." This phrase was first used by Pope John XXIII in his encyclical "Pacem et Terris" in 1963. It was later developed in the Vatican II document, Gaudium et Spes, or the Pastoral Constitution on the Church in the Modern World.

"To carry out such a task, the Church has always had the duty of scrutinizing the signs of the times and of interpreting them in the light of the Gospel."[21]

And what is the task that requires this scrutiny? This is found in the preceding paragraph:

"the Church seeks but a solitary goal: to carry forward the work of Christ under the lead of the befriending Spirit."[22]

For the Church to remain aligned with the will of Christ and the Holy Spirit, we must become keenly aware of the world around us and the Spirit among us. Jesus promised his spirit would remain with us, accompanying the Church through history. The Spirit of God exists now, in our present time. This Spirit, as Gaudium et Spes says, wants to befriend and be in relationship with each of us as a human community. This befriending Spirit is nothing less than the Spirit of God.

---

[21] Gaudium et Spes, 4.
[22] Ibid, 3.

God is not a removed force, an absent clockmaker who acted once and left, but a God who is immediately and passionately in relationship with us, desiring our salvation. Salvation history is not an ancient story about a God who acted way back when but a God acting now. The ethos of this Spirit can be known, wants to be known, and we can participate in this Spirit. The Spirit of God is one of compassion, justice, peace, reconciliation, and unity amid diversity. How can we know this? Because this is the driving agenda and focus of Jesus in the Gospels and of God that emerges in the Jewish scriptures as well. Salvation history is still happening. It is not just history. The story of God's abiding love for God's people is unfolding today as well. If we have eyes, ears, and hearts to perceive it, we can align our communities, wills, and actions with the living Spirit.

The Spirit of the living God is also present throughout all of creation. God cannot be limited to only one place, group, or person. God is God, all in all. Therefore, God is present "whenever two or more are gathered in His name."[23] God is also present in all the affairs of humanity,

---

[23] Matt 18:20

in our political processes, our social movements, our industry and recreation, our homes, our schools, our workplaces, and on the sidewalks and highways. God is present in all of creation, in the birth, death, and renewal of the natural world, in the chaos and order of the entire cosmos, and in the tiniest and seemingly insignificant microcosm. Communities of faith exist to be agents of the God that is everywhere and in all things. At our baptism, each of us is commissioned as agents with a charge to keep an eye out for the presence of this God in our journey and to be an active participant in bringing the Spirit of compassion, justice, and mercy to every inch of God's creation.

Scrutinizing the Signs of the Times is an act of faith and belief. It is a belief that God is there. God is here. God is waiting for us to notice and respond; when we do, we grow closer to God. We become friends and collaborators with the Spirit, but we can only respond well when we see. Reading the Signs of the Times is not a guessing or wishing game. How many times in the Gospel does Jesus warn us against being willfully blind or deaf, not seeing clearly, or having our ears closed to the truth? Reading the Signs of the Times requires a sober look at reality to see the brokenness in the world, our cities, our neighborhoods, our institutions, our families, and ourselves. It also means looking hopeful for the credible signs of Christ's presence in the world. We keep our eyes open for signs of compassion and those working for justice. We befriend those who practice mercy and reveal a love beyond boundaries.

Reading the Signs of the Times also means looking critically at our communities to see where we fall short of our professed belief. This can be a complex reflection, but it is necessary to convert our communities. We must see where we exclude others, where we perpetuate injustice, and where our practices are more aligned with other spirits of competition, greed, fear, superiority, or jealousy. When our communities are unreflective and do not practice reading the Signs of the Times in our lives and the world around us, it is easy to fall into practices and beliefs that unwittingly lead us astray of the Spirit of God in our midst. Reading the Signs of the Times keeps us connected to the living Spirit of God. As individual disciples and communities of faith, we learn to notice, then we know to open our hearts to the brokenness around us, and finally, we respond in new ways. We become agents of God and friends of Christ when we begin to see the world through the lens of the Gospel. Then, our parish communities become schools of seeing, training centers where disciples learn to hear the cry for justice and mercy and work together to find creative and impactful ways to be the presence of Christ in a broken world.

Parish Application – Creating a Parish Census

A parish census is much more than simply a count of the number of people attending mass in your parish. It is a tool to ascertain valuable information about your parishioners, compare your parish membership to the general population in your parish geography, and, when seen through the lens of mission, identify priorities for ministry within your parish and broader community outreach efforts.

The results of the parish census application described here can be used in various venues to assist parish leaders in focusing their plans to address the community's needs. The reports generated from the census can be used as a reflection tool within a broader communal discernment process, like the parish assembly and spiritual conversation process described in the next chapter. It can also be used by parish pastoral councils, finance councils, and parish staff to drive the goals and objectives of their ministerial plans. Finally, parish census reports can help to identify shared needs among parishes in a particular area and by diocesan ministers as they develop resources to assist parishes.

The process described below provides a single snapshot of the life of a faith community. As such, it is limited in that it is like taking the temperature of a community at one moment. When this process is undertaken annually, additional insights can be gleaned as the community changes over time. This type of longitudinal study can be beneficial when developing pastoral plans to address emerging needs within the community.

The parish census process described below is meant to create a portrait of the parish community in relationship to the broader community.

Sources of Data

Various sources of data are drawn together to create the final report. These sources include:

- In-pew parish survey
- US Census report of the parish boundaries
- Sacramental data

Parish Survey

The parish survey or census is a process that gathers information directly from each parishioner. The survey can include demographic information such as age, gender, race, educational attainment, household income, language spoken at home, length of residency, etc. In addition, information regarding parishioners' history with the parish can be gathered, such as length of time at the parish or sacraments received. This information is collected through a data collection tool administered by parish leaders. The following section provides information on several methods for conducting this data.

US Census

The US Census collects information every ten years and provides annual reports on specific data points. Considering this decennial schedule, consider when the last census occurred and how this might impact your data report. As much as possible, when creating comparison reports, the rule is to match "apples with apples," if you cannot make a perfect match, articulate these discrepancies clearly.

When creating a comparison report between the parish and broader communities, select the census blocks co-terminus with the parish boundaries. Next, select questions from the census that you want to ask the parishioners and use the exact wording of the census question in the parish survey. Again, apples to apples.

You can use comparison information when providing the final report to the broader parish. However, also be aware that some information creates the need for further mission-focused reflection, such as the percentage of the community living in poverty or alone. The parish has a responsibility to serve everyone in the parish boundaries.

Sacramental Data

Each parish must submit sacramental data to the diocese for use in the official Catholic directory and diocesan record keeping. Since this information is collected annually, creating a longitudinal study of sacraments is easy. For instance, how many baptisms were celebrated this year, last year, five years ago, or fifty years ago? Each parish must keep these records on the premises and in perpetuity. Therefore, a longitudinal study dating back to the parish's founding is possible.

Comparing the reception of sacraments to one another and longitudinally looking at them can reveal necessary information about the parish. Examine the number of children baptized in one year compared to the number of children that received their First Communion 8 years later or their confirmation years after that. This kind of study can offer information on the transience or mobility of parishioners. Another vital consideration is comparing the number of baptisms and those received into the parish to the number of funerals. To state it a bit crudely, how many parishioners are coming in compared to those going out? If funerals are greater than baptisms and RCIA candidates consistently year after year, this is an essential consideration for vitality.

Preparing a Parish Survey

The first question to consider when developing a parish census is what you want to know. A plethora of information can be gleaned by only asking a few questions. Different data points can be combined to focus the reflection on various community portions. For example, consider a basic in-pew survey taken at each mass that asks only the age, gender, zip code, and length of residency of each mass-attending parishioner. This information can determine the age breakdown of each mass and the generational breakdown of all men or women. It could be used to determine how far people travel to your parish, if there is a specific mass that people from outside the parish boundaries tend to be attending, and if their age or gender is a factor in their choice of mass. All of this is from only 3 points of data.

The questions that we asked for the Brooklyn Parish Census included 15 questions. These questions were lifted word for word from the official US Census. As a result, we were able to create a profile of the worshipping community and situate those results next to the exact profile of the general population in the area. The combined reports then revealed information such as parishioners' average annual household income compared to others in the neighborhood. If parishioners' race, gender, age, educational attainment, primary language, and length of residency were similar to or different than those in the neighborhood. This helped identify differences that could create a barrier to participation and inclusion. Since our survey was located in a large metropolitan area, we also looked at those who lived alone or with non-family members and those who lived with spouses and children. We then looked at the age of those living alone and with non-family members to identify if these were young professionals living with roommates or older adults living alone or in institutional settings. All of this information assisted parishes in their discernment and development of relevant mission-based initiatives. So, the first question in developing a parish census is to find out what you want to know and what you think you do not know but need to know to be more effective in your ministry.

If your planning team or pastoral council is still determining what you want to know and what might be relevant, look at a census report from the US Census Bureau for your city or even a census block in your area. The US Census Bureau has an extensive website to access information about your community. See what the Census asks and consider how that information about parishioners and your parish geography's general population might be helpful.

Creating the Census Survey

Once you know what you want, the next step is creating your survey. Many tools can be used to collect survey information. You can use a simple index card if you ask for 4 data points or less. Golf pencils will be needed if a paper survey is being conducted. Using different color cards for each mass is an easy method to code mass times. Cards of a single color are distributed at each mass with the pencils. Each family can complete one card. They are asked to write their zip code in one corner and the ages and gender of each person in the family in the other corner. This is also an opportunity for people to write their email in the remaining corner if they want to be on the parish mailing list.

Technology has made survey-taking much easier. SurveyMonkey is an excellent website that will help you create the survey, collect the information, and compile the information into usable reports with applicable charts and graphic representations of your data. SurveyMonkey also provides a link and generates a QR code for parishioners to access the survey. This can be very useful for in-pew surveys, which will be discussed below.

Preparing the Parish for the Parish Survey

A parish census or survey is usually conducted as part of a broader pastoral planning initiative in the parish. A planning initiative is a campaign with a beginning, a progression, a culmination, and a conclusion. If this is the case, the collection of information either through personal encounters, interviews, consultations, or surveys is meant to serve as further steps in the planning process. When presenting the parish census to parishioners, it should be conveyed that this data collection exercise is part of the parish's wider planning process. There must be some feedback loop or follow-up to any data collection to avoid frustration or possible cynicism. The method of pastoral planning is meant to be as transparent as possible. Asking for information and never providing a report on the data results will make members hesitant to participate again.

Therefore, the first public step in a data collection campaign is informing all parishioners early and often that the data collection will happen. The process of informing parishioners does not need to be extensive, but it is best if it is repeated weeks before the survey. These announcements in the bulletin or from the pulpit are an opportunity to engage parishioners further in the planning process. The announcement can stress that the pastoral council seeks to create the most accurate and complete picture possible. This is only possible if every parishioner participates and is included. The various forms of subjective consultation gathered through conversation and personal interviews are also important, but survey data provides a macro view of the entire community. The results of this data will provide a lens and a mirror for the parish community to reflect upon to sharpen their observations and confront their actual reality. Parish leaders foster participation and buy-in when they promise to share the survey results with parishioners and invite comments.

Survey Weekend

Ideally, the data collection occurs on a single weekend at all masses. Other options can be provided for homebound parishioners or those who might be away from the parish that weekend. However, collecting the data during the weekend liturgies ensures the greatest possible response. While some may find the interruption to be an inappropriate break in the liturgical celebration, bringing data collection into the context of liturgy denotes its centrality and importance. Data collection is a step in a Spirit-led communal discernment process that includes the participation of all. The community is coming to know itself more deeply for the explicit purpose of co-creating a mission-driven plan to proclaim the Gospel in word and deed into the future. Learning who we are and responding to that reality is a part of *liturgia*, literally the work of the people, a work that must be open and inclusive to be relevant.

The survey, either in paper or electronically, is shared with all parishioners. The best time for this is directly after the homily. The pastor can explain the process or invite a pastoral council member to facilitate the process. If using paper, the ushers can distribute cards or sheets, or they can be placed at the ends of the pews before the mass. Pencils will also be needed. The cards or sheets can be collected with the regular collection or as a second collection period. Alternatively, a QR code can be created for an electronic data-gathering process. A small sheet with the QR code can be attached to the back of each pew or printed in the bulletin. Parishioners can use their phones to access the survey. The entire process takes between 5-7 minutes to complete. The musicians might play some instrumental music while parishioners take the survey.

Creating Data Reports

Once the data is collected, it is tabulated and converted into charts, graphs, and tables that can quickly convey the results. If a paper survey is used, this process will require some tabulation. First, a different color card or sheet is used for each mass. This is an easy way to identify the mass time. An Excel spreadsheet can be easily created to chart each point of data. Once the data is inputted into a spreadsheet, Excel can create charts and graphs to represent the data. These images can easily be copied into a presentation format.

If using an electronic format, the program or app, such as SurveyMonkey, will do most of the heavy lifting. It will tabulate the data and create graphic representations of the data as well.

Additional steps are required if you create a report comparing information from the parish to the local neighborhood. It would be best if you first determine your parish boundaries. Every parish has a geographic boundary, and the pastor and community are responsible for caring for the souls in that geographic region. While parish boundaries are not necessarily followed by many mass-attending Catholics who travel from outside the boundaries to attend, the pastoral plan should focus on outreach and evangelization to those within the boundaries and those who travel in. The US Census website can provide information down to the level of a census block. A primary step in developing a parish report is determining which census blocks are within the parish boundaries. The parish boundary is only sometimes coterminous with the census blocks, so a prudential choice must be made regarding which blocks to include.

Once the census blocks are determined, create a report on the designated area based on the questions you have included in the parish survey. The census data is inserted in one column in the spreadsheet, and the parish data is inserted in the next. It will then be possible to create charts to compare these data sets.

Using the Reports

The parish survey results are shared with all parishioners in the spirit of transparency and openness. This can be a central focal point for a parish-wide consultation or assembly. This gathering is the main focus of the parish's planning process. The data collection weekend is an opportunity to remind people of the coming gathering when the results will be shared. In addition, one or two of the most striking points in the data might be shared either verbally or in the bulletin. Different data points could be shared each week leading up to the planning gathering.

At the parish assembly or planning gathering, a complete data presentation is offered by a member or members of the parish pastoral council. Significant data points can be discussed and explained, but the presenter should refrain from drawing conclusions from the data. This is a critical point. The purpose of the planning gathering is to gather the reflections of each parishioner. This can be influenced and manipulated if parishioners are told precisely what each data point means by the presenter. It reduces the interpretation of the data to a single perspective and then asks parishioners to respond to that perspective instead of the data itself. Allow parishioners to draw conclusions, discuss those observations, and reflect on their meaning together.

Chapter Eight
Engaging Everyone
A Parish Communal Discernment Process

There was electricity in the air at St. Sebastian's parish center in Woodside, Queens. The newly reformed Parish Pastoral Council had been preparing for this gathering for months. Council members had been sharing reflections on the parish's mission for the past two months, focusing parishioners on the essential areas of the parish's life and consistently inviting parishioners to this evening of engagement. Flyers and notices, bulletin announcements, banners, and reminders from the pastor spread the word that all were welcome and encouraged to join in this critical conversation on the life of the parish. A hospitality team had arranged the parish hall with round tables and chairs, a screen and projector, and a prayer space in the center. Facilitators and notetakers had been trained, and a leader from the council had been preparing their opening remarks.

Just before 7:00 pm, parishioners began to enter the hall, passing by a history board displaying pictures of deceased parishioners, former pastors, and the faces of the past that shaped the story of this faith community. Everyone checked in and received their table assignments. The tables were arranged in various colors, one color for each primary language group in this multi-cultural community. The tables were split between English-speaking and Spanish-speaking, with a few in Polish and even one in Chinese.

Once everyone had gathered, the pastor opened the evening with a welcome and prayer and turned it over to the council, who had created this space for consultation and engagement. Parishioners had received the parish data report and a series of questions about two weeks before the assembly evening and were encouraged to reflect and pray over the material before attending. A council member reviewed the data reports, pointing out some critical areas of concern. Another member reviewed the central elements of the parish's mission – creating a lens through which parishioners were encouraged to look at the life of their community. With the help of a council member or facilitator, each table engaged in a conversation around the reflection questions. They listened deeply to one another as the individuals at the table became a collaborative group seeking the way that the Holy Spirit was inviting them to respond to the challenges they faced and the mission they were about. Notes on each of the conversations were created. Each individual offered their notes, and a collective table response was created. Each table had an opportunity to share one or two points that emerged.

The meeting was only two hours long, but parishioners left feeling more deeply connected, heard, and incorporated into the parish's future.

Theological Reflection -The Theology of We

Communal discernment within a parish community has two main goals. The first is to discern God's will and the Holy Spirit's call. The second goal is to use this moment of discernment to deepen the relationship between and among parish members and strengthen the sense of connection at the heart of a faith community. In other words, communal discernment is a cruciform experience where we deepen our vertical relationship with God while simultaneously stretching and reinforcing our horizontal relationships with one another.

The parish is a privileged place where individuals come together as a community to live in unity while simultaneously retaining and celebrating the diversity of members. A gathering or assembly of all parishioners may initially seem unwieldy or logistically impossible, but a committed team can navigate these practical elements. The parish pastoral council fosters community and participation of all parishioners in and through a planning conversation.

Pope Francis, when calling for universal participation in the local consultations as part of the Synod on Synodality in 2021, offered a Latin maxim to guide this process: *Quod omnes tangit debet ab omnibus approbari* (What affects all should be discussed by all.) While this maxim originated in Roman law, theologically broad participation in the discernment of a faith community's future recognizes that the Holy Spirit is moving in the hearts of every community member, and the community's decision will be better informed if everyone has an opportunity to share their insights, especially insights that emerge from their prayer.

Secondly, full participation in a collective decision-making process shares the goal of encountering and converting the members. Broad participation leads to better decision-making as leaders develop a more profound sense of the community and parishioners develop a greater understanding of ownership in decisions. In addition, offering spaces for mutual listening, collaborative discernment in identifying the presence of the Spirit in the community, and collective wrestling with the concerns and possibilities facing the parish provide a space for engagement that can deepen connections, ignite zeal and hope, and rescue many from alienation and quiet resignation. Such discernment is also a training ground demonstrating the Catholic belief that Christ is alive and God is present in the community. Christ seeks a relationship with all disciples to inform our experience and lead us towards the fullness of our individual and communal life. The Christian community is called to be more and more a reflection of Jesus and the first Christians who relied on the presence of the Holy Spirit to guide their decisions in all things.

Through communal discernment opportunities, parishioners learn how the practice of prayer, reflection, deep listening, silence, speaking from the heart and experience, and naming the movement of the Spirit in a collaborative group marked by vulnerability and a mission-focus can be a powerful exercise in their discipleship. It is a practice that leads us closer to God. Communion, participation, and mission move a community from an assembly of many individuals to a community of We. The methods and practices that the parish community uses to decide its future direction reflect what we believe about each person and God.

We say we are a community of faith, that God speaks to all hearts and seeks a relationship with all, and that everyone matters and is welcome. Opportunities to participate in the decision-making processes of the parish through communal discernment is a concrete way to live out these beliefs. In contrast, we live a cruciform life informed and reliant on the horizontal and vertical relationships that define a Christian community.

Parish Application – Evening of Communal Discernment

An Evening of Discernment is the culminating experience of a parish communal discernment process and leads to developing a parish pastoral plan or goals. The gathering follows a deliberate preparatory period of data gathering, reflection, prayer, and reflection by all in the community. The meeting is an opportunity for the pastor and parish leaders to provide an open space for encounters among parishioners focused on the collaborative goal of discerning the will of God for their community. As such, it is a communal spiritual practice where the community, grounded in a belief that the Spirit of God is present among them, engages in deep listening and attentiveness to what the Holy Spirit is trying to reveal.

The primary goal of an Evening of Discernment is to gather insight and input from parishioners and all stakeholders that will inform the goals and priorities of the parish. Such input could be collected in various ways, such as through focus groups or surveys that do not require such a large gathering or full participation. However, while more efficient and less work, such methods must address the deeper goals of communal discernment. Communal discernment is meant to provide an experience of mutual encounter among disciples within a community to build solidarity and communion. Also, communal discernment demonstrates the full participation of all members and incorporation into the community. Suppose communal discernment is seen as the Tent of Meeting where God meets us and shares God's intent for us. As such, a parish assembly that encourages the participation of all is a sure way to Enlarge the Space of Our Tent in a way that includes the voice of all and teaches that everyone matters and has something important to contribute.

The pastor presides over the assembly and remains the chief discerner, while the parish pastoral council facilitates comprehensive listening and reporting.

Organizing and preparing for a parish assembly is best undertaken through a division of labor. Several organizing groups can be developed from among the pastoral council members. Each group has a set of responsibilities that culminate into a successful parish-wide consultation. The groups and responsibilities follow. When preparing to plan an Evening of Discernment, the council is organized into the following groups:

Hospitality Group

This group is responsible for the space where the parish gathering will occur.

Duties include:

- Securing an ample space (i.e., Parish Hall)

- Arranging for round tables or circles of chairs with about 6-7 people at each table/circle
- Providing nametags, notepaper, pencils, and index cards for recording responses
- Arranging projector and screen for presentations
- Providing/Arranging refreshments for break
- Create and manage the registration process for participants
- Commissioning an inter-generational group to create a history display with pictures, artifacts, and memorabilia of the parish. This can be arranged as a display near the entrance of the space. In this way, participants walk through the history of the parish into the meeting space, where they will discuss the future.

Publicity Group

This group is responsible for advertising the event and arranging pulpit talks. Duties include:

- Creating publicity for the evening and disseminating in bulletins, websites, announcements for parish groups, outreach to non-practicing parishioners

- Introduce the discernment questions to the community, inviting all to pray and reflect on the questions in anticipation of the assembly— model prayer and reflection on the question through pulpit talks and at existing parish groups.

- Facilitate pulpit talk scheduling. Parish Council members offer a brief 2-minute pulpit talk each weekend liturgy for several weeks before the discernment. The council member (re) introduces the question that will be discussed at the gathering, shares a brief reflection on it from their personal experience as a parishioner, and invites all to attend the discernment. Group members help to prepare a schedule and coach each member on their presentation.

Process Group

This group leads the process for the gathering and organizes the small group conversations. Duties include:

- Establish agenda

- Facilitates discernment process

- Ensure that presenters are prepared. Presentations include a summary overview of the data reports, a report on themes emerging from individual conversations that may have occurred before the assembly, and an explanation of the process for conversation and the next steps.

- Elicit and train conversation facilitators for each table. The best method for training facilitators in spiritual conversation is through experience. This could be accomplished by using other processes in this book and offering to teach others by inviting them to participate in a conversation and reviewing the facilitator's role with them directly after experiencing a conversation.

- Consider how notes will be taken during the discernment. Notetakers can be identified for each table, or one person from the table can be named.

- Prepare and offer prayer for the meeting.

Data Group

The data group is responsible for compiling and collecting data from various sources and presenting the data to the community as part of the communal discernment process. Duties include:

- Facilitate the parish survey process (see Ch. 7)
- Collect sacramental data from parish records
- Prepare data presentation report
- Implement a strategy to share data with parishioners in advance of the Evening of Discernment
- Provide a brief recap presentation of essential points of data at the discernment evening

Preparatory Calendar

The following is a sample calendar outlining the preparatory steps to be completed before the Evening of Discernment. This calendar is only a suggestion. As the council and pastor develop their timeline, the following may be helpful.

Eight weeks out

- Publicity Group prepares publicity pieces, including bulletin announcements, fliers, online promotional material
- Hospitality Group reserves the space, secures the number of tables needed, and sets up a registration site or process
- Data Group conducts the parish survey

Six weeks out

- Process Group recruits small group facilitators. One facilitator is needed for every 5-6 participants.

Four weeks out

- Publicity Group and pastor introduce questions that will be used in spiritual conversations and encourage individual parishioners to begin to pray and reflect on the question.
- Data Group compiles survey results and prepares data reports

Three weeks out

- Hospitality group begins to create nametags

- A pulpit talk by a council member given on the preparatory reflection process
- Process group holds facilitator training (experience of spiritual conversation)

Two weeks out

- Process group develops prayer for the assembly
- Data Group delivers data presentation and disseminates data report

One week out

- Hospitality Group – Buy/prepare refreshments, Prepare registration list
- Process Group – Create table assignments and coordinate with the hospitality group
- Data Group – Finalize brief data presentation and test projection if used

The Evening of Discernment Agenda

The parish assembly can be completed in about 2.5 hours in a single evening. The event focuses on a Conversation in the Spirit that is convened at each table simultaneously with the assistance of a facilitator. The event is meant to be a prayerful encounter among parishioners to work collaboratively through listening and reflection to discern the Will of God for the parish community. The following is a sample agenda to provide an overview of the activities and flow of the assembly.

Evening of Discernment Agenda

6:00	Parish Council members arrive for final review of the agenda and final preparations.
6:15	Facilitators arrive. Receive their table assignments
7:00	Pastor welcomes all. Introduces Assembly Facilitators.
7:10	Opening Prayer
7:20	Facilitators provide overview of goals and agenda, provides brief overview of conversation process and provide questions

7:40	Data presentation given by Data Group members
7:50	Break
8:00	Facilitator reintroduces question and initiates small group conversations
8:10	Conversations in the Spirit in small groups
9:00	Each table provides one or two points of convergence that emerged in their conversation
9:20	Facilitators discussed next steps in the process
9:30	Pastor thanks all for participating and offers final blessing

Small Group (5-7) Conversation in the Spirit Process

- Facilitators welcome all and restate questions, establish an order of speakers
- Begin **Question One**:
- **Round One**: Each participant has 4 minutes to share a reflection on the question that has emerged from their prayer and reflection
- One minute of silence after all speak
- **Round two**: Each participant has 2 minutes. What struck you and moved you while you were listening to others?
- One minute of silence
- Begin **Question Two**:
- **Round one**: Each participant has 4 minutes to share a reflection on the question that has emerged from their prayer and reflection
- One minute of silence after all speak
- **Round two**: Each participant has 2 minutes. What struck you and moved you while you were listening to others?
- One minute silence

- **Round Three**:
- Based on our conversation and your reflection, how and in what ways do you believe the Holy Spirit is calling us to act and respond?

A Note on Notetaking

Recording the salient points from the spiritual conversations is a critical task. Notes ensure that the fruits of the conversation become part of the larger discernment process of the parish. Submitted notes should include the results of the third and final round of conversation, noting points of convergence, in which people agreed, and points of divergence, where there was disagreement and any points of consensus. Notes on the second round could be recorded as well. Notes on the first round are rarely recorded. A notetaker can be designated for each table. The notetaker could be one of the group members or a separate individual for only this role. The facilitator should be someone other than the notetaker.

Next Steps

Following the Evening of Discernment, notes should be gathered, recorded in an electronic format (such as a Google Drive document), and shared with all participants for their reflection. A Pastoral Council meeting is held soon after the discernment. The Council can engage in spiritual conversation regarding their reflections on the notes, asking again where the Holy Spirit is calling them. A prayer over the responses is also encouraged as this is the intermingled voice of the Spirit and the People of God.

The result of this synthesizing and clarifying conversation is to develop mission-focused goals. These goals include how the parish can live into its mission in new ways. However, these goals do not yet need to specify actions. A second round of conversations addresses specific steps. These goal groups are focused brainstorming opportunities to consider ways that the goal can be concretely implemented. The results of these brainstorming conversations are sent back to the council again. The council and pastor finally articulate objectives that will help them achieve the articulated goals. Eventually, lead agents are named to lead the implementation of each objective. Council members should not be named as objective implementers. The goal is to empower and lift up new leaders in the community to implement the plan. During the implementation phase, council members act as supporters, coaches, mentors, and resource providers to leaders implementing various objectives.

Spiritual Conversations can again be convened one year after implementing goals or objectives. These conversations can serve as an evaluation exercise. Such conversations focus more on what went well and what could be improved. They are focused on the way that the mission of the parish has been lived out and in what ways. The conversation invites participants and leaders to share their experiences of the implementation and how they and others have been impacted. The summaries of these conversations then shape a conversation between the pastoral council, pastor, and goal or objective leaders about ways to continue and improve the implementation of the goal.

Chapter Nine
Putting it all Together
A Discernment Year

The six practices outlined in this book are designed to stand on their own within the life of the parish. Each practice models a different means of engaging the parish community and the living Spirit in discerning God's will. The applications are designed to model different approaches to discernment for individuals and the community. Yet, these practices and applications link together to shape a journey of deepening engagement designed to embed spiritual discernment as a constitutive exercise in the life of the parish and each disciple. In this way, the parish becomes a school of discernment, or, as St. Pope John Paul II said, "a school of communion."[24]

The curriculum for a school of discernment and communion is grounded in engagement at each step. These practices of discernment deepen the relationships that parishioners have with one another and with God, both individually and as a community. This will also lead

---

[24] Novo Millenio Inuente, 33.

to new ways of decision-making. It will always be easier for one positional leader to make unilateral decisions. Processes of discernment, especially those that involve the entire community, will always take longer to complete and will require more deliberation and consideration. Therefore, efficiency in decision-making is not the pre-eminent value.

Discernment slows decision-making, but other values and gifts come to the fore. Transparency, open participation, and active listening foster presence and conversion through witness, collaboration, ownership, shared responsibility, and consensus, which brings people along instead of imposing decisions. Ultimately, success in discernment is measured in participation and deepening relationships, both horizontal and vertical.

The parish applications in the previous chapters can become a concerted campaign to shape a faith community rooted in the values and practices of discernment and engagement. The applications are intentionally ordered to move from simple to complex, individual to communal, and I to We. Engagement and discernment are journeys of spiritual growth.

The practices in this book are a curriculum of experiential learning intended to shape a culture of communion and participation focused on mission. Therefore, a staged implementation plan is recommended to lay the groundwork for each consecutive practice. Each parish will be unique in its application and engagement and may find that some practices are more applicable or appropriate for their community. Below is an example of a parish plan to implement all six practices over 18 months.

September	Introduce "Where have you met God lately" Continue until Advent
October/November	Form core group for Breaking Open the Word
Advent	Introduce BOTW to community Core group members facilitate
February/March (Lent)	Discernment for PPC New Members

Easter season	1:1 Conversations Parish Survey
Summer	Continue existing initiatives/Plan for Assembly
September/October	Hold Conversation Assembly
November/Advent	Parish Plan is disseminated

Whether you choose to implement one of these discernment exercises or a comprehensive pastoral planning process, may the practices in this book, developed over decades of experience both by me and those who taught me, become doorways to more robust relationships among members of your faith community and a deeper relationship with the God who calls us all and always to mission.

Appendix I

Discernment Night Process
for Selecting Parish Pastoral Council Members

The Discernment night is typically held one week after the Information night. The entire Discernment session is couched in the context of prayer, specifically, prayer to the Holy Spirit for guidance. A facilitator who will guide the people through the process must be chosen beforehand. The worship aid in Appendix II explains the process. This can be distributed to all participants.

Environment

As soon as people enter the room, it should be clear that this is very different from the Information Night. The room should be very purposefully arranged. Participants should sit in chairs set in a circle. The facilitator also sits in the circle.

A small table sits in the center with a cloth that reflects the current liturgical season. The table contains a candle, a Bible, a crucifix, or other symbols. This creates an environment of prayer and is also important so that those who may be more reserved have a point of concentration when speaking.

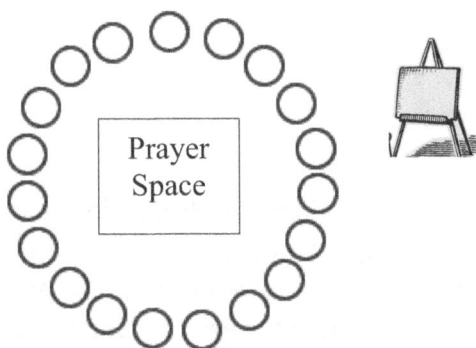

Process

The worship aid in Appendix II incorporates all the steps of discernment. One of the nominees read the reading. The facilitator or the pastor conducts the opening prayer and should include a prayer invoking the Holy Spirit to be with the group. The faith-sharing question is done in the large group. After stating the question and encouraging others to share their ideas, there will be a time of silence. It is normal, and someone will speak eventually. Not everyone needs to speak, but leave enough time so those who wish to speak have an opportunity.

- Participants must be continually reminded that we are looking for the Holy Spirit to guide the group in discerning the gifts (not the people) needed at the table. This helps to depersonalize the process so that everyone is affirmed.
- Faith Sharing allows people to view this process in light of the gospel and begin to talk to each other openly and honestly. It would be helpful to remind the group that while those being discerned will be asked to respond to questions later on, faith

sharing is not mandatory, and it is open to all in the room who wish to respond.

Questions

- In Part I, the questions are straightforward. Anyone can begin and then continue around the circle in order. As people answer, take note of their names. Then, after each person speaks, the facilitator guides the group in the affirmation so that each person is prayed for after speaking. The night should follow a prayerful pace but must also keep moving.

- Part II and III questions form the heart of the discernment. The role of the facilitator is to ensure each person being discerned has the opportunity to respond. The facilitator should accept what was said and ensure that people refrain from responding or beginning a dialogue over what someone has shared.

Discernment

You will need a blackboard or newsprint for the consensus process.

- First, ask if anyone would not like to continue in the process. Those not wanting to be considered for selection should make themselves known. They may still participate in the selection, though, by naming others.

- The process must be transparent. This means that while silent ballots may be more comfortable for those present, it is recommended that the affirmation of gifts be done aloud. Go around the room and ask each person to name three people whose gifts they feel are needed at this time on the council.

    i. Interestingly, transparency also helps ensure a compassionate discernment. As participants witness the process unfold, people's gifts are affirmed that may not have been in a silent ballot, and participants who might have chosen themselves will rarely, if ever, choose themselves verbally. In a transparent process, people's focus moves outward as they consider others.

- Each selected name should be written once on the newsprint. When the name is repeated, place a mark next to it until you have a list of names with marks.

- Once there is a list of names, ask those present to state what they see emerging. If consensus is clear, circle those names that emerge, ask for the group's permission to move forward, and pray over those discerned. If one person clearly emerges but others do not, circle the emerging name/s and continue to another round of affirmation.

- The second round repeats the process. Begin with a blank newsprint sheet. Go around the circle in the opposite direction as the first round. Anyone can be named except those who have already been selected. Again, check for consensus.

- The caucus: While rare, a facilitator may face no apparent emergence between two or three names in certain circumstances. It is often helpful for the facilitator to pre-arrange with the pastor flexibility on the number being discerned. Often, a pastor will be willing to accept an additional PPC member if there is an impasse. However, if this is not the case, the facilitator may ask the remaining 2 or 3 individuals to move to another room away from the group, asking those remaining to pray for guidance.   Once outside the room, ask them to decide who will be discerned. They should affirm to each other those gifts they see in each other that could benefit the council and come to a determination. The facilitator should ensure they understand their task and leave them to do this. If the caucus lasts more than 10 minutes, the facilitator should return to check in with them.

- Additional option- If names do not emerge naturally, and the group cannot reach a consensus, consider placing the names in a chalice or a basket. Far from considering this a random selection, make it clear that we are asking God to show the group what they need to see, to reveal to them the name that eludes them. Ask for the guidance of the Holy Spirit, choose a symbolic representative, perhaps the person who has been on the PPC the longest, and ask for the affirmation of everyone in the room before having that person choose the name.

- Once the council members are selected, announce the names and ensure someone has a list. The final prayer is included in the worship aid. The sign of peace ends the evening. Thank everyone for their participation.

Appendix II

Discernment Night
For Parish Pastoral Council

Invitation to Prayer

Leader: Come, Holy Spirit, fill the hearts of your faithful

All: And kindle in them the fire of your love.

Leader: Send forth your Holy Spirit and they shall be created

All: And you will renew the face of the Earth.

Reading (Romans 12)

Now I urge you: do not conform yourself to this age, but be transformed by the renewal of your mind, that you may discern what is the will of God, what is good and pleasing and perfect. For by the grace given to me I tell all of you not to think of yourselves more highly than you ought to think, but to think soberly, each according to the measure of faith that God has apportioned. For as in one body we have many parts, and all the parts do not have the same function, so we, though many, are one body in Christ and individually parts of one another.

Since we have gifts that differ according to the grace given to us, let us exercise them: if prophecy, in proportion to the faith; if ministry, in ministering; if one is a teacher, in teaching; if one exhorts, in exhortation; if one contributes, in generosity; if one is a leader, with diligence; if one does acts of mercy, with cheerfulness.

Let love be sincere; hate what is evil; hold on to what is good; love one another with mutual affection; anticipate one another in showing honor. Do not grow slack in zeal; be fervent in spirit and serve the Lord. Rejoice in hope, endure in affliction, persevere in prayer. Contribute to the needs of the holy ones, exercise hospitality. Have the same regard for one another; do not be haughty but associate with the lowly; do not be wise in your own estimation. If possible, on your part, live at peace with all.

The Word of the Lord

All: Thanks be to God

Reflection
(Faith sharing is open to all attendees)

Of all the advice Paul gives us, was there a line or phrase that stood out to you or was significant to you in some way? Why?

Discernment Process

Those being considered to fill the role of council member are asked to address several questions without judgment, interrogation, or interruption by others. Respectful listening and continuing prayer to the Spirit marks this time.

Part I

Each person introduces themselves. Candidates should include the following information:

- Name
- Length of time as a member of the parish
- Ways in which they have been involved in the parish over the years
- The church activity, ministry, or service they found most rewarding

After each person speaks, the group affirms and prays for them.

Leader: Let us pray in gratitude for the life of _____ and all the gifts s/he has already shared with this faith community. May God continue to lead him/her in discipleship and service of God's people.

All: Amen!

Part II

Each person being discerned answers the question:

What gifts do you bring to the ministry of parish pastoral councils?

Part III
Each person chooses one of the following questions to answer:

146

What one thing do you think would make the biggest difference in the spiritual life of our parish?

What one thing do you think is the greatest need in the parish?

If you could give all the people of our parish an injection of some spiritual gift, what would it be and why?

Now that all have spoken, this is the time for questions and answers, if there are any.

At this time, people may withdraw their names for consideration, although if you do, you are invited to stay with the group and participate in the discernment.

Each person is asked to identify individuals whose gifts would contribute to the council. Then, briefly discuss the reasons for their choice.

Closing Prayer

Leader: Let us pray:

In gratitude for your presence among us, O Holy Spirit, we give you thanks and praise. Now bless these your servants as they assume the ministry of leadership in our community. Give them unity, vision, wisdom, and a great love for you and your people. We ask this in the name of Jesus, our model and our pastor, now and forever. Amen.

Reader: (2 Cor 9:1, 11-15)

Now, about your service to God's holy ones, I know your eagerness. You are being enriched in every way for your generosity, which through us produces thanksgiving to God, for the administration of this public service is not only supplying the needs of the holy ones, but is also overflowing in many acts of gratitude.
Through the evidence of this service, you are glorifying God in your fidelity to the Gospel of Jesus Christ and the generosity of your contribution to God's people and to all others. In prayer for your good, they hope in you because of the surpassing grace of God. Thanks be to God for such an indescribable gift!
The Word of the Lord.

All: Thanks be to God

Leader: We pray now in the words that Jesus gave us: Our Father...

May almighty God bless us, the Father +
and the Son and the Holy Spirit

All: Amen.

Leader: Go in peace, to love and serve the Lord in one another.

All: Thanks be to God.

Leader: Let us conclude with a greeting of peace.

Appendix III

Sample Bulletin Announcements
for Discernment Process

Sample #1

Dear Parishioners,

In a few short weeks, the parish will hold nominations for additional membership on the Parish Pastoral Council. The council is a visioning and planning body of parishioners who foster full participation of the entire parish in the life and mission of the church as lived out in _____ Parish. In consultation with the Pastor, the Parish Pastoral Council actively listens to and identifies the needs and concerns of the people and reviews the parish pastoral plan to respond to these needs. The Council also seeks to implement the plan by involving parishioners.

We need ## parishioners who have these qualities:

- a desire for spiritual growth in themselves and the Parish
- enthusiasm about the future of the Parish
- a willingness to listen, to speak honestly, and to work toward consensus

- the ability to inspire and empower others to delegate
- flexibility and openness with people and ideas

Nominations will take place on the weekend of _____ at all masses. Those identified as nominees will be invited to attend an information night on _____. At this session, all nominees will learn about the role of the Parish Pastoral Council. After this evening, all will be asked to reflect and pray on this information and discern whether or not they feel called to this ministry of service and leadership. The following week, on _____, a formal discernment night will be held. The community will bless the new pastoral council members on _____. Please pray for the guidance of the Holy Spirit.

Sample #2

Last week, nominations were held at all the masses, and individuals identified who might be potential candidates for the Parish Pastoral Council. These parishioners have been sent an invitation to come to the

Information Session on _____. At this

session, all nominees will learn about the role of the Parish

Pastoral Council. After this evening, all will be asked to

reflect on this information and discern whether or not

they feel called to this ministry of service and leadership.

The following week, on _____, a

formal discernment night will be held. Let us all continue

to pray for the guidance of the Holy Spirit throughout this

process.

Sample #3

Dear Parishioners,

Following the "Information Night" held this past

_____ Night, all those who attended were asked to

reflect and pray on the information they received

regarding the role of the Parish Pastoral Council. They

were also asked to prayerfully discern whether or not they

feel called to this ministry of service and leadership on the

pastoral council. This _____, a formal discernment

night will be held. Here, all those who feel called to this

ministry will return. These individuals will be asked to

address several questions regarding their gifts and feelings about the parish's life and future. The entire night is done in the context of prayer and reflection. By the end of the evening, the group will discern who would be best suited for membership on the Parish Pastoral Council. I ask you to keep all those involved in this process in your prayers throughout the week.

Sample #4

Dear Parishioners,

Last _____ night, the final discernment process for the Parish Pastoral Council was held. Through this evening of prayer and reflection, those nominees who returned after the Information Night listened to one another and finally, using a consensus process, chose ## from among them who they felt had the gifts needed for membership on the Parish Pastoral Council. The names of the new Parish Pastoral Council members are as follows:

____

I also wish to thank those members of the Parish Pastoral Council who will be leaving the council after _____. Their involvement and dedication to this vital ministry of leadership have been a great asset to me and our parish. Those members who will be going off Council are as follows:

Thank you for your commitment to this ministry and our parish.

The newly discerned members of the Parish Pastoral Council will be commissioned at the ##:## mass on _____. Thank you for your consistent prayer during this discernment process. May the Holy Spirit continue to guide the good work of our Parish Pastoral Council.

Appendix IV

Parish Pastoral Council Nomination Form

Our parish needs leaders to help guide our pastoral life and growth. Please help identify persons with the leadership gifts that are required at this time.

Leaders should have the following characteristics:

- The desire for spiritual growth in themselves and the parish
- Enthusiasm about the future directions of our parish
- Willingness to listen, to speak honestly, and to work toward consensus
- The ability to inspire and empower others and to delegate
- Flexibility and openness with people and ideas

To be considered, a parishioner must:

- be a baptized Catholic
- have been a registered member of our parish for at least two years
- be a participant in the ongoing worship life of our parish
- be at least twenty years old

We need XX new members for our council. Please list the names of parishioners you identify as having the gifts for pastoral council leadership.

I suggest inviting the following individuals to consider leadership ministry through service on our Parish Pastoral Council.

_____

_____

_____

Appendix V
Commissioning Ceremony for New Council Members

The commissioning ceremony usually takes place within Mass following the homily. If there is already a Parish Pastoral Council, begin with A. If an entirely new Parish Pastoral Council, go to B and omit the words in square brackets.

Sample A

Presider: I invite those who have completed their term of office on our Parish Pastoral Council to come forward. (*Names of outgoing members are read out as they come forward.*)

Presider: On behalf of our parish, I would like to thank you for your contribution to the work of the Parish Pastoral Council. Please accept this token of our appreciation, and may you continue to respond generously to your baptismal call by serving others.

Presider hands each person a gift and invites the congregation to offer a round of applause.   He then gives each member a lighted candle.

Sample B

Presider: You have worked to bring the light of Christ to our parish. The ministry now passes to others. I [now] invite those chosen to serve our community as [new] members of the Parish Pastoral Council to come forward.

Names of [new] PPC members are read out as they move towards their places on the sanctuary, facing the people. The priest stands to one side:

Presider: Each of you has been called from this Parish community to serve as a member of the Parish Pastoral Council. Do you accept the responsibilities of parish leadership that we place on you?

PPC members: We do.

Presider: Will you strive to be more like Christ so that you will be better able to serve his people?

PPC members: We will.

Presider: May God bless and sustain you in the work you have taken on for this parish community. Be a beacon of light in the life of the Church.

Christ is the light of the world. Your task is to walk in the light of Christ and to share it with others. *(Omit if it is a new PPC)* The light that has been tended by these former members of the Parish Pastoral Council now passes to you. May this candle remind you of our mission to let the light of Christ shine out for all to see.   *(The outgoing members of the PPC (or the presider, if it is a new PPC) present a lighted candle to each new member, saying:* **Let your light shine before all.**

The outgoing members now return to their places.

New members:

We are grateful for your trust in us and accept this ministry within our community.
We pledge ourselves to serve you with joy, love, and enthusiasm.

We will work to help to build the life of the Christian community in our Parish and Diocese.

We will try to be conscious of the needs of all parishioners and to make Christ present for everyone, following his example as one who served.

We ask for your prayerful support, encouragement, and insights as we commit ourselves to serving this community.

The priest invites the congregation to show their support in a round of applause. The new members then return to their places.

Intercessions

The Prayers of Intercession might include a Prayer for the Pastoral Council members and their families and for the grace to lead with dignity and courage.

A prayer of thanks for the work of the outgoing members might also be included.

Appendix VI

Checklist for the Selection Process for Parish Pastoral Council Members

Preliminary

- Determine how many PPC members will be discerned
- Decide methods of publicity and possible creative options
- Create a bulletin announcement (which includes all dates)
- Make enough copies of Nomination forms for all parishioners at each Masses
- Make sure pencils or pens are available for nomination forms
- Post Nomination Form online with a QR code and link on the parish website
- Create a pulpit announcement to describe the process

Nomination Weekend

- Place nomination forms and pens/pencils in every pew for each Mass
- Describe nominations from the pulpit (Provide deadline)
- Provide time for parishioners to fill out nomination forms
- Post QR code in pews if using the electronic nomination option
- Ushers collect forms (not unlike a second collection) or boxes left in the back of the church

Post-Nomination

- Review all nomination forms and select those to be invited to the information night.
- Mail out invitations for Information Sessions (or phone calls)

Information Session

- Arrange chair set up
- Hospitality (Coffee, snacks)
- If the PowerPoint session is used, set up the laptop and projector beforehand
- Ensure all outlets are accessible and extension cords are available if needed

Discernment Night

- Arrange chair set up
- Create prayer space
- Provide easel/newsprint and marker

Bibliography

New American Bible. Revised Edition. Washington, DC: United States Conference of Catholic Bishops, 2011.

"Apostolicam Actuositatem." In *Vatican Council II: The Conciliar and Postconciliar Documents*, edited by Austin Flannery, 1-32. Northport, NY: Costello Publishing Company, 1996.

Code of Canon Law: Latin-English Edition. Washington, DC: Canon Law Society of America, 1983.

"Dei Verbum." In *Vatican Council II: The Conciliar and Postconciliar Documents*, edited by Austin Flannery, 49-86. Northport, NY: Costello Publishing Company, 1996.

"Gaudium et Spes." In *Vatican Council II: The Conciliar and Postconciliar Documents*, edited by Austin Flannery, 903-1033. Northport, NY: Costello Publishing Company, 1996.

"Lumen Gentium." In *Vatican Council II: The Conciliar and Postconciliar Documents*, edited by Austin Flannery, 350-426. Northport, NY: Costello Publishing Company, 1996.

Pope Francis. *Evangelii Gaudium: Apostolic Exhortation on the Proclamation of the Gospel in Today's World.* Vatican City: Libreria Editrice Vaticana, 2013.

Pope Francis. "Speech at the 50th Anniversary of the Synod of Bishops." Vatican City, October 2015.

Pope John Paul II. *Novo Millennio Ineunte: Apostolic Letter at the Close of the Great Jubilee of the Year 2000.* Vatican City: Libreria Editrice Vaticana, 2001.

Acknowledgments

I am incredibly grateful to all the teachers and mentors who have shared their passion for ministry, discernment, and pastoral planning with me and entrusted me to carry on the great work they began. I am most grateful to Mary Ann Gubish and Susan Jenny for introducing me to parish pastoral planning and the ministry of the parish pastoral council and for allowing me to incorporate some of their material into this book.

I am thankful for the support, mentorship, and friendship of Dr. Barbara Sutton, Marti Jewell, Mark Mogilka, Ellen Rhatigan, Bill Pickett, Rick Krivanka, Dr. Robert Miller, Jim Barrette, Rev. Msgr. Jim Lang, Terry Ginther, David DeLambo, Dr. Brad Hinze, Mark Fischer, and all the members of the Conference of Pastoral Planning and Council Development.

I am also grateful to the pastors and parish pastoral council members who trusted me and allowed me to serve them and their faith communities over the past 25 years. It has been the honor and privilege of my life to serve you and share in the Great Commission.

Thanks also to my Breaking Open the Word group at St. Francis Xavier parish, who showed up every Saturday morning during the pandemic to share faith.

Finally, thanks to Rose, who never doubted what the Spirit had in store.

Made in United States
Cleveland, OH
06 June 2025